Winning Government Grants and Contracts for Your Small Business

Winning Government Grants and Contracts for Your Small Business

Mark Rowh

McGraw-Hill, Inc.

New York St. Louis San Francisco Auckland Bogotá
Caracas Lisbon London Madrid Mexico Milan
Montreal New Delhi Paris San Juan São Paulo
Singapore Sydney Tokyo Toronto

Library of Congress Cataloging-in-Publication Data

Rowh, Mark.
Winning government grants and contracts for your small business / Mark Rowh.
p. cm.
ISBN 0-07-054142-6 : —ISBN 0-07-054143-4 (pbk.) :
1. Small business—United States. 2. Grants-in-aid—United States. 3. Public contracts—United States. I. Title.
HD2346.U5R69 1992
658.15'224—dc20 91-28088
CIP

1 2 3 4 5 6 7 8 9 0 DOC/DOC 9 7 6 5 4 3 2 1

ISBN 0-07-054142-6 {HC}
ISBN 0-07-054143-4 {PBK}

The sponsoring editor for this book was David Conti, the editing supervisor was David E. Fogarty, and the production supervisor was Pamela A. Pelton. This book was set in Baskerville. It was composed by McGraw-Hill's Professional Book Group composition unit.

Printed and bound by R. R. Donnelley & Sons Company.

To Dave and Teresa Smith, the kind of friends everyone hopes for, but few are lucky enough to find

Contents

Preface

This book is written for anyone in the small business sector interested in applying for grants or contracts from government agencies. Both those now in business and those considering starting a business should find this information helpful.

No special credentials are needed to pursue the activities suggested. Good writing skills are a plus for anyone working in proposal development, as is flexibility in thinking, but no special training or background is necessary.

It is important to note the spirit in which this book is offered. Advertisements in newspapers, magazines, and other media too often make unsubstantiated claims about funds that are available to start or help small businesses. They make it seem as if one need only know the right address or telephone number to get thousands of dollars from government sources with no strings attached (and, of course, there is usually a fee for this supposedly lucrative data). *Winning Government Grants and Contracts for Your Small Business* is *not* this type of source.

Government grants and contracts *are* available for small businesses, but not as handouts to anyone who asks for them. Rather, most such awards are made on a highly structured, competitive basis. This book provides an overview of government programs which make grant and contract awards and ways small firms can successfully compete for them. Small businesses win millions of dollars in contracts and grants every year. If you are interested in pursuing such funding for your small business, *Winning Government Grants and Contracts* is designed to provide just the help you need to get started with this exciting alternative for business development.

Acknowledgments

The author greatly appreciates the cooperation of the following in the development of this book:

U.S. Department of Energy

U.S. General Services Administration

U.S. Department of Health and Human Services

U.S. Small Business Administration

National Science Foundation

National Aeronautics and Space Administration

Mark Rowh

Winning Government Grants and Contracts for Your Small Business

1
Dollars Available

If you want to make your small business more successful or get a new business off the ground, here's something you should know: money may be available from the government to help you. This does not refer to loans or to shady, "get-rich-quick" schemes. On the contrary, funds may be available which

1. Are perfectly legitimate.
2. Need never be repaid.
3. Are available not just to nonprofit organizations but also to those in the private sector – including small businesses!

The truth is that thousands of small businesses have obtained such funds through grants and contracts awarded by the U.S. government and governmental entities. Enterprising businessmen and women have, as a group, received billions of dollars every year from government agencies through grants and contracts for special projects and activities.

We're not talking here about procurement contracts based on providing goods or services to the government, although such awards also represent great potential (as discussed in a later chapter). Rather, project grants and contracts are usually based on a less well known but often lucrative process whereby applicants propose specific projects or activities in which the government has an interest. For those proposals that are accepted, the result is a grant or contract award which can go a long way toward making any business successful.

Examples of such possibilities for small businesses include:

- The Small Business Innovation Research program, which sponsors research projects related to forests, production or protection of plants and animals, rural development, and many other issues.
- The U.S. Department of Energy's Energy-Related Inventions program, which makes grants to help inventors launch businesses based on energy-related products.
- Programs sponsored by the Department of Labor under the Job Training Partnership Act, through which businesses may receive grants to provide job training for the unemployed or underemployed.
- Various programs providing grants and contracts to minority firms, including some offered by the Small Business Administration.
- A wide range of contracts offered on an *ad hoc* basis (that is, to address specific needs which may arise). For example:

  The Federal Highway Administration recently solicited bids for the design of bridge deck drainage systems.

  The Agriculture Department sought firms to train participants from developing countries in pest management.

  The Department of Labor requested proposals to develop a project on youth training and employment issues.

  The Department of Education invited proposals for a project to conduct a national assessment of progress in providing education about American history.

  The Federal Highway Administration sponsored a project to examine the needs of older male and female pedestrians (the contract for this project was offered only to applicants who were small businesses as a special "small business set-aside").

  The Centers for Disease Control requested proposals for development of a mathematical model of the transmission of Lyme disease.

  The National Endowment for the Humanities, in a small business set-aside, solicited proposals for development of a video for promotion of humanities education.

  The U.S. Army Corps of Engineers, in another competition open only to small businesses, announced plans to issue a contract for an investigation of historical and prehistorical resources in the Pacific Northwest.

  The Department of Health and Human Services invited proposals from small businesses to evaluate the effectiveness of projects aimed at preventing drug abuse and gang activity.

Small Business Administration
U.S. Department of Agriculture
U.S. Department of Education
U.S. Department of Energy
U.S. Department of Defense
U.S. Department of Health and Human Services
National Aeronautics and Space Administration
National Endowment for the Arts
National Endowment for the Humanities
National Science Foundation
U.S. Information Agency
U.S. Department of Labor U.S. Department of Transportation

NOTE: Many of these large agencies contain individual offices or programs which conduct their own grant or contract programs. For example, the Department of Health and Human Services includes the Public Health Service, the Food and Drug Administration, Health Resources and Services Administration, National Institute for Occupational Safety and Health, National Institutes of Health, and others.

Figure 1-1. Some federal agencies that award grants or contracts.

Such contracts and grants in a variety of business areas are offered by many different government agencies. When combined with programs offered on a continuous basis and those initiated by new legislation, the result is a host of funding possibilities for small businesses. Figure 1-1 lists just some of the federal agencies which make grant or contract awards.

In addition to federal agencies, other units of government also make grant and contract awards. State governments, municipal governments, and other governmental entities also provide funds through the grant and contract route. Opportunities and procedures vary from one area to the next and among different agencies, but many of the principles involved in pursuing federal funding also apply in obtaining awards from other levels of government.

How Awards Are Made

The kinds of funds discussed here are not distributed by the government on an unsolicited basis but must be sought. In most cases, contracts and grants for special projects are awarded on a competitive basis.

Although conventional wisdom might hold that such awards are controlled by politicians who use their influence to steer money toward their friends and supporters, in reality the process is often truly competitive. Most government programs have been designed to be as fair as possible, with every applicant having an equitable chance at receiving funds. In most cases, this is how awards are made:

- First, the funding agency issues a Request for Proposals (RFP), which is an open invitation for any eligible party to submit an application for funds. The RFP includes the basic information needed to compete for a grant or contract award (a sample Request for Proposals is provided in Appendix D).
- Next, applicants complete written proposals which must provide information specified in the RFP. These usually must be submitted by a specific date.
- Each proposal is judged against preset criteria, earning a quantitative score (for example, a proposal might receive an average score of 84 out of a possible 100 points, as scored by three different readers).
- Those proposals earning the highest point totals receive the awards. Thus a major consideration is not just identifying such programs but learning how to prepare competitive proposals. Later chapters provide the information needed to develop successful proposals.
- Organizations receiving government funds carry out the activities proposed in their applications, in many cases acquiring new skills and experience which in turn lead to new grant or contract awards.

Benefits to Businesses

Why would small businesses be interested in winning government awards? In many cases, funds provided by grants and contracts can provide the extra financing necessary for success in today's competitive environment. It is important to realize that a grant represents free money—it need not be repaid, ever. The activity supported by a grant can help a new company get started, or help an existing one strengthen itself considerably. Similarly, a contract to conduct specific work can provide funds for personnel, equipment, or other resources to help business enterprise succeed.

Here are just a few examples of awards that small businesses have received:

- The Mac Tech Company of Chelmsford, Massachusetts, landed a contract from the U.S. Department of Education to develop a wheelchair-type vehicle for handicapped people who not only cannot walk but are also blind.
- Stoddard-Hamilton Aircraft of Arlington, Washington, received a contract from the National Aeronautics and Space Administration to develop lightning-management technology for smaller general-aviation aircraft.
- A number of small businesses across the country have received awards through the Job Training Partnership Act to provide training for disadvantaged youth, dislocated adult workers, and others needing job training.
- Emerson and Stern Associates, a small company based in San Diego, has received multiple awards from the Department of Education, Department of Transportation, National Science Foundation, and other agencies for software research and production in speech and language programming.

These companies and others like them have found that government funding is by no means the domain only of huge defense contractors or other large corporations. On the contrary, small businesses can compete successfully for government awards in many fields.

In reviewing the opportunities provided to small businesses through research and development awards, the National Science Foundation has listed the following seven advantages that federal funding offers:

1. Knowing in advance the size of the market and the level of profit to expect
2. Having security that work will be paid for
3. Having a customer demand cycle which does not ebb and flow with the general business cycle in commercial markets
4. Having a virtual guarantee that allowable costs will be paid
5. Having the ability to structure payments for cash flow and tax purposes
6. Having the ability to allocate parts of overhead and fixed costs to contracts
7. Having the ability to receive payment for conducting work with potential commercial applications

Certainly, research funding represents one of the most exciting areas of potential for small businesses, and those firms specializing in research and development are among the most likely candidates for federal funding. If your firm has scientific or engineering capabilities, seeking grants or contracts may bring enormous opportunities.

At the same time, small businesses specializing in many other areas may also qualify for government funding. Research awards are far from the "only game in town" as far as federal funds are concerned. To determine if your small business has potential in this area, ask yourself these questions:

- Does my company address areas which the government has shown interest in developing?
- Can I identify a significant problem or need which my company might help solve?
- Does my firm have the capabilities of meeting the standards expected of grant or contract recipients?
- Would a grant or contract award be consistent with future plans for the development and expansion of my company?
- Does my business provide products or services which government agencies might be interested in purchasing, even if my organization is not a likely recipient of a special purpose grant or contract?
- Can I or someone in my company develop the skills needed for successful proposal development?

If you can answer yes to some or all of these questions, then you might want to explore the possibilities provided by federal funding.

Grants versus Contracts

Throughout this book, information and advice will be provided about both grants and contracts. These two terms are often used somewhat interchangeably, but in a strict sense there are several basic differences in the two.

Perhaps the most important difference is in the expectations of the funding source. In most cases, *grants* are given to organizations or individuals with the understanding that, in essence, nothing is expected in return. The recipient may be asked to provide reports and other information to prove that funds were used for the purposes described in the proposal, but that is all. The funding source generally does not expect the grantee (the recipient of the grant) to provide a product or the equivalent as payback for receiving the award.

With most *contracts,* on the other hand, the award is more of a business deal than a gift. The government wants something done, so it enters into a contract with one or more organizations or individuals to accomplish the desired work. This may involve conducting research, providing a service, or some other activity. But the end result is that the recipient of funds is expected to provide the government with some type of product or service either during the funding period or at its conclusion.

In a broad sense, many grants might be seen to represent social interests, while contracts exist more in the business domain. Many grants are outgrowths of congressional legislation or other actions designed to address particular concerns of society. Because of their prevalence in the nonprofit sector, one might assume that grants are available only to nonprofit organizations. This is true for many grant programs, but many others are also open to businesses. For grant programs open to profit-making firms, achieving the overall program goals is most important, not what type of organization receives funds to help meet these goals. If a small business can get the job done, no problem.

For example, say Congress reacts to the need to provide wider educational and career opportunities for physically disabled people and passes a law mandating that more such opportunities be provided. As a part of the legislative package, a new grant program is authorized which includes funds for special educational programs for the disabled. After the law has been passed, funds are authorized, regulations written and published, and a grant competition announced.

To carry this example further, say that eligible applicants include public schools and other nonprofit organizations, but the competition is also open to proprietary (profit-making) schools and businesses which are interested in establishing special training programs. A small business which provides tax preparation services, for instance, might then apply to conduct a short-term training program to teach disabled people the basics of tax preparation. The company receives funds for this purpose, conducts the program, and then also benefits by having trained people available to fill job openings. The result is that individuals have benefited, the small business has received a financial boost as well as a source of personnel, and society's need to help the disabled find jobs has also been addressed.

A typical *contract,* by contrast, may have as its goal a specific accomplishment. For instance, the U.S. Justice Department may want to develop a system for keeping national statistics on juvenile crime and data on related criminal justice matters. The Justice Department issues a request for proposals for the development of such a system, allowing both public agencies and private businesses to apply. The main concern is the ultimate product, and the successful applicant must be able to deliver this product (a workable statistical system) by the conclusion of the funding period.

Grants and contracts may also feature some technical differences. The format for a typical grant proposal differs from that of a proposal for a contract (more details about format are provided in subsequent chapters). Reporting requirements may also vary. (There is often greater interaction between project personnel and agency officials in carrying out contracts.)

Differences in grants and contracts as described above are the rule, but sometimes distinctions between the two become blurred: A grant may include the development of some type of product as its goal, or a contract may lack a specific product (in research, the research itself may be both the means and the end). Where appropriate, the following chapters will differentiate more fully between the two. At the same time, it is important to note that much information about competing for government funds can be applied to both grants and contracts. The reader is invited to adapt all information provided to any funding scenario.

Proceeding from Here

If the process of seeking grants or contracts seems complicated, don't worry. It can be mastered by virtually anyone willing to learn the ground rules and take the necessary steps to submit competitive proposals.

The next chapter provides an overview of one of the most promising funding programs for small businesses. Chapter 3 shows you how to locate information on potential funding sources. Chapters 4 and 5 cover the elements of proposals and how to submit them. Chapter 6 addresses the basics of grant and contract budgeting. The administration of funded programs is discussed in Chap. 7, while Chap. 8 provides tips on the development of important relationships with people in the funding agencies. Chapter 9 provides information on procurement contracts and how to pursue them. Chapter 10 suggests ways of taking advantage of the availability of government funds. After reviewing this material, you could be well on your way to landing a significant grant or contract award for your business!

2 The Small Business Innovation Research Program

Before proceeding to the how-to of pursuing grants and contracts, it will be helpful to look at what may be the premier program of this type for small businesses. This program can be particularly attractive to smaller firms interested in research and development. Certainly all grant programs do not support research projects, and firms which do not conduct research can still seek funds from a variety of other sources, as noted in Chap. 1 and elsewhere in this book. But for today's growing number of small businesses with research capabilities, the program described below can offer tremendous potential.

Help for Innovative Projects

The Small Business Innovation Research (SBIR) program is a special government effort to help small businesses carry out research and development projects. The program has two overall goals: to foster development of new products and processes by small companies with a high-

The information in this chapter is based on "Small Business Innovation Development Act," Seventh Annual Report of the Small Business Administration's Office of Innovation, Research, and Technology, July 1990.

tech emphasis and to increase the number of resulting processes and products that are brought to the commercial marketplace. The emphasis is on helping small businesses operated by the disadvantaged and members of minority groups.

Since the initiation of the program in fiscal year 1983, small businesses have received more than 14,000 awards totaling over $1.8 billion. In 1988–89 alone, small businesses landed nearly 2,900 awards worth over $431 million.

The SBIR program was created by Congress when it passed the Small Business Innovation Act in 1982. The intent was to strengthen the role of small businesses in government-sponsored research and development. The act's four major purposes were:

- Stimulating technological innovation
- Using small businesses to help meet federal research and development needs
- Encouraging participation by minority and disadvantaged people in technological innovation
- Increasing private sector commercialization innovations derived from federal research development

Under this program, any federal agency that awards research and development contracts and grants totaling more than $100 million a year must set aside a certain percentage (up to 1.25 percent) for awards to small businesses. These agencies include:

Department of Agriculture

Department of Commerce

Department of Defense

Department of Education

Department of Energy

Department of Health and Human Services

Department of Transportation

Environmental Protection Agency

National Aeronautics and Space Administration

National Science Foundation

Nuclear Regulatory Commission

In addition, several agencies with research and budgets of more than $20 million but less than $100 million are required by the law to establish goals for small business set-asides. Their goals must be no lower than the total amount the agency awarded to small businesses during the previous fiscal year. These agencies include the following:

Department of the Interior

Department of Justice

Department of the Treasury

Department of Veteran Affairs

Agency for International Development

Smithsonian Institution

Tennessee Valley Authority

Types of Awards

The SBIR program supports two types of awards. Phase I awards support research projects with a major goal of testing the feasibility of an idea and its technical and scientific merit. Awards average $50,000.

Phase II awards are fewer in number but greater in size. They allow projects with high potential to continue developing the basic concept or practice for one or two years. Phase II awards can be as large as $500,000 or more.

Phase III allows the company to bring its innovation into the marketplace, but SBIR funds are not given for this purpose. Instead, support from the private sector is encouraged. In some cases, Phase III activity can lead to eventual production contracts with federal agencies.

Over 11,000 Phase I awards have been received by small businesses since the SBIR program began. More than 3,000 Phase II awards have also been made. See Table 2-1.

The numbers and amounts of grant awards should give you an idea of the overall promise this program holds for small businesses, but it

Table 2-1. Awards to Small Businesses under the SBIR Program

Cumulative total, 1983–89

Number of Phase I awards	11,366
Number of Phase II awards	3,537
Total number of awards	14,903
Total dollars awarded	$1.821 billion

SOURCE: Office of Innovation, Research, and Technology, U.S. Small Business Administration.

may also be helpful to look at several instances where small businesses have succeeded thanks to the SBIR program:

- Eastern Technical Associates, of Raleigh, North Carolina, won SBIR awards through the Environmental Protection Agency to develop new ways of measuring smoke emissions from smokestacks.
- Photonics Technology, Inc., of Northwood, Ohio, has made major advances in the development of high-definition television (HDTV) thanks to SBIR awards from the National Aeronautics and Space Administration.
- NPI, a small business located in Salt Lake City, Utah, has received several SBIR awards for development of a genetic tree extract. The product has been used in applications ranging from insect control to preservation of foods.
- Coherent Research, Inc., of Syracuse, New York, has used SBIR funds to develop computer hardware and software designed to boost the capacity of computers for information processing.
- NeoRx Corporation, of Seattle, Washington, has received SBIR funds to conduct research related to cancer detection and treatment.

Small firms such as these have found that SBIR awards provide an infusion of funds for projects which may not have been possible otherwise. These awards have aided the growth and development of many small companies.

SBIR funds support work in a variety of technical areas. See Table 2-2.

No matter where you live, it is possible to obtain SBIR funding. In fiscal year 1989 alone, such awards were distributed as follows:

California	674 awards for a grand total of more than $97 million
Virginia	157 awards for a total of more than $23 million
New York	151 awards totaling over $18 million
Texas	113 awards for more than $14 million

Companies in every state in the United States (as well as Puerto Rico) have received SBIR awards. It is not necessary to be located in Silicon Valley or some other area famous for technological development to compete successfully under this program. Rather, projects are selected on the basis of merit and potential impact.

Table 2-2. Major Technological Areas Supported by the SBIR Program

Computer, information processing, analysis
- Computer and communication systems
- Information processing and management
- Signal and information processing
- Systems studies
- Mathematical sciences

Electronics
- Microelectronics
- Electronics device performance
- Electronic equipment and instrumentation
- Electromagnetic radiation propagation
- Microwave and millimeter-wave electronics
- Optical devices and lasers

Materials
- Advanced materials
- Materials processing and manufacturing
- Coatings, corrosion, and surface phenomena
- Materials performance
- Fundamentals and instrumentation

Mechanical performance of vehicles, weapons, facilities
- Hydrodynamics
- Aerodynamics
- Acoustics
- Mechanical performance of structures and equipment
- Control
- Mechanical measurements

Energy conversion and use
- Transport sciences
- Propulsion or combustion technology
- Large scale energy usage
- Energy conversion, electric power

Environment and natural resources
- Ocean science
- Atmospheric sciences
- Water management
- Earth sciences
- Environment protection

Life sciences
- Medical instrumentation
- Biotechnology and microbiology
- Behavioral sciences
- Physiology and miscellaneous

SOURCE: Office of Innovation, Research, and Technology, U.S. Small Business Administration.

How to Apply for Funds

To pursue SBIR funding, take the following steps:

1. Write to the following address and ask that your name be placed on a mailing list to receive SBIR information:

U.S. Small Business Administration
Office of Innovation, Research, and Technology
1441 L Street, N.W., Room 500
Washington, DC 20416

2. Once you start receiving materials, review them for possible follow-up. Documents called "pre-solicitation announcements" should be particularly helpful. These quarterly publications provide a wealth of information and reduce the need to review information provided by individual agencies.

3. If you decide to apply, follow the tips provided in Chaps. 4, 5, and 6 to develop the best possible proposal.

3
Locating Funds

Half the battle in acquiring government funds is knowing where to look for them. But anyone can find the needed information by consulting the right sources.

As previously noted, most grants and contracts are offered through a competitive process. This begins when the funding agency issues a Request for Proposal (RFP) or announcement that it intends to award funds and is seeking applications. The RFP will include a date by which applications must be submitted. Any application which meets this deadline, assuming that it comes from an eligible organization or individual, will be considered for funding.

To make sure that every citizen or group has equal access to this process, government agencies make their RFP's public by announcing them in publications known to provide this kind of information. These publications will provide the details you need to pursue grants and contracts.

You can also learn about the availability of grant funds by setting up an informal network with others who are similarly interested. And you can have your name placed on mailing lists to receive application packets and other information about various government programs. As with other areas of endeavor, knowledge is the key. The more you learn about grants and contracts and the more involved you become, the more information will flow your way.

Key Publications

As mentioned above, the most practical way to identify potential funding sources is to review publications which announce requests for applications or describe ongoing funding programs. This will involve an investment of time or money or both, depending on whether you subscribe or use copies available in libraries. In any case, even a minimal investment can pay off many times over if just one grant or contract award results from your efforts.

Fortunately, a number of publications provide the basic details needed to pursue grant and contract possibilities. In fact, providing such information has become an industry in itself, especially in the case of newsletters and directories that cater to the nonprofit sector but which also can be useful to small businesses. Here are some of the most widely used of these publications.

The *Federal Register*

A key source of information is the *Federal Register,* which is published by the federal government. This is one of the most voluminous periodicals around, averaging more than 50,000 pages a year. It is issued every weekday, except for holidays, by the Office of the Federal Register, National Archives and Records Administration in Washington, DC. The publication is available in most college and university libraries (many of which are open to the public) as well as large public libraries and other organizations. It can also be ordered from the Superintendent of Documents, U.S. Government Printing Office, Washington, DC 20402. The most recent costs for a year's subscription were $195 in microfiche form or $340 for paper editions. The *Register* is also available on magnetic tape for $37,500 a year, but that may be a bit expensive for most small businesses.

The content of the *Federal Register* varies widely. Its overall purpose is to provide a uniform system for making available to the public regulations and legal notices issued by federal agencies. These include presidential proclamations, executive orders, various federal agency documents required to be published by act of Congress, and other government documents of public interest. Among these are proposed federal regulations which might affect businesses or other organizations, as well as announcements of upcoming grant competitions.

Using the *Federal Register* can be both exasperating and rewarding. The document is full of fine print, acronyms, bureaucratic language, references to legislation, and other complex language typical of government publications. At first glance, it might appear that only an attorney could use or understand this publication, but on closer reading most sections become understandable. The format includes several standard headings and subheadings printed in boldface type, making it relatively simple to skim through the document and find relevant information. This is rendered easier by a table of contents arranged by name of federal agency. Say your business specializes in new types of solar heating devices. To see if any new grants are available in this area of interest, you might look under Department of Energy, National Science Foundation, and a few other headings in the table of contents, and read farther only if a subheading indicating a grant announcement is listed. If not, this research will have taken only a few moments of your time. If on the other hand an announcement of potential interest appears, it will provide the initial details needed to decide if an application from your company might be a good idea. This will include a description of the program, what kind of awards will be made, criteria for selection, and where to obtain application materials.

Figure 3-1 is a sample page from the *Federal Register* which includes part of an actual grant announcement for which private businesses were eligible to apply.

Commerce Business Daily

The single most important source of information about potential contracts is *Commerce Business Daily*. Published by the U.S. Department of Commerce on a daily basis except Sundays, this publication lists not only opportunities to compete for special-purpose contracts but also those for procurement of goods and services (see Chap. 9 for information on procurement contracts).

Commerce Business Daily is designed to provide information to the public in such a way that any qualified business or other entity will have a chance to compete for certain types of government contracts. For example, government agencies intending to initiate procurements of $10,000 or more are required to have advance notice of their intent published in *Commerce Business Daily*.

This publication also includes notification of contracts that have recently been awarded (which can be particularly helpful in assessing funding trends in different agencies) as well as other information such as details on surplus property sales, subcontracting possibilities, and opportunities to conduct business with firms outside the United States. It does not report on classified projects, demands for perishable goods, services for educational institutions, and a number of other special topics.

A typical entry in *Commerce Business Daily* identifies the broad category of demand (for example, services) and then more narrowly defined areas (such as accounting or financial or architectural services). The agency in question is listed along with its address, followed by pertinent information about the need being listed. This will include a multidigit solicitation number which should be included in any corre-

1516 **Federal Register / Vol. 56, No. 10 / Tuesday, January 15, 1991 / Notices**

meeting of the conference, as well as the annual meeting to be held next July (a noti:e will be published in the **Federal Register** prior to such meeting), brings together enforcement officials, other govern.nent officials, and representatives of business, industry, trade associations, and consumer organizations to discuss subjects that relate to the field of weights and measures technology and administration.

Pursuant to section 2(5) of its Organic Act (15 U.S.C. 272(5), the National Institute of Standards and Technology acts as a sponsor of the National Conference on Weights and Measures in order to promote uniformity among the States in the complex of laws, regulations, methods, and testing equipment the that comprises regulatory control by the States of commercial weighing and measuring.

DATES: The meeting will be held January 13–17, 1991.

LOCATION OF MEETING: Hyatt Regency Bethesda Hotel, Bethesda, MD.

FOR FURTHER INFORMATION CONTACT: Albert D. Tholen, Executive Secretary, National Conferences on Weights and Measures, P.O. Box 4025, Gaithersburg, Maryland 20885. Telephone: (301) 975–4009.

Dated: January 10, 1991.

John W. Lyons,

Director.

[FR Doc. 91-943 Filed 1-14-91; 8:45 am]

BILLING CODE 3510-13-M

National Oceanic and Atmospheric Administration

[Docket No. 901104-0304]

National Status and Trend Program; Request for Proposals and Availability of Financial assistance

AGENCY: Office of Oceanography and Marine Assessment (OMA), National Ocean Service, National Oceanic and Atmospheric Administration (NOAA), Commerce.

ACTION: Notice of availability of financial assistance.

SUMMARY: For FY91 NOAA/OMA intends to carry out research projects addressing aspects of the National Status and Trend Program (NS&T). In particular, we are interested in the study of the historical contamination of the coastal United States using sediment cores. OMA is issuing this notice describing the conditions under which applications will be accepted and how OMA will determine which application will be funded.

DATES: Pre-proposals should be received by 22 February 1991 and full proposals by 3 May, 1991.

ADDRESSES: Information and applications should be directed to: Dr. Nathalie J. Valette-Silver, NOAA, N/OMA32, 6001 Executive Boulevard, room 312, Rockville, MD 20852, Tel: 301–443–8655; FAX No: 301–231–5764.

SUPPLEMENTARY INFORMATION:

I. Introduction

The United States Congress has authorized the National Oceanic and Atmospheric Administration (NOAA) to conduct a broad range of marine environmental research, development and monitoring activities. One statutes specifically authorize marine environmental quality monitoring. The National Ocean Pollution Planning Act of 1978, 33 U.S.C. 1701–1709 states that NOAA shall "establish within the Administration a comprehensive, coordinated, and effective pollution research and monitoring program", 33 U.S.C. 1704. The NS&T Program was initiated to fulfill, in part, these mandates.

The aim of the NS&T Program is to quantify the concentrations of key contaminants in the Nation's coastal and estuarine environments and to measure their biological effects. The data acquired using a nationally uniform set of sampling and measurement techniques are used to determine temporal changes and spatial patterns in marine environmental quality.

II. Funding

The NS&T Program is anticipating having up to $400,000 per year for this research. However, there is no guarantee that sufficient funds will be available to make awards to all approved projects. For FY91, the exact level of funding is presently unknown.

III. Program Goals and Priorities

This request for proposals (RFP) represents the initial step in a multi-year, coordinated, interdisciplinary and interinstitutional research program aimed at reconstructing historical contamination of the U.S. coastal and estuarine systems using sediment cores.

In the past, several historical studies have used cored sediments because sediments are recognized to be good long term integrators of many toxic contaminants. However, most of these studies were performed in the late 1970s to the early 1980s. Since the late 1970s, many changes have occurred in the Federal and state laws governing the disposal of pollutants in the environment. New data from cored sediments are needed to trace the effect of these recently imposed restrictions. The NS&T Program is designed to acquire data that will help in assessing temporal trends in the coastal and estuarine sediment contamination.

To support this multi-year research program, NOAA/OMA anticipates having up to $400,000 to study each year 3 to 4 estuarine/coastal areas. Each year, new estuaries or coastal areas will be selected. Financial Assistance obtained through this RFP for a given geographic area, will be for 16 months maximum. Future or continued funding will be at the discretion of NOAA based on such factors as satisfactory performance and the availability of funds. However, if some Principal Investigators (PIs) are able to study more than one area of interest, they will have to submit different proposals for different areas and will compete with the other applicants for the available funds.

To simplify administrative management one PI has to be responsible for the total project in each geographical area. Consequently, it is recommended that scientists wishing to submit proposals in response to this RFP collaborate in order to get dating, trace elements and organic compounds analysis for one geographical area coordinated in a single proposal.

States, universities, non-profit, or for profit organizations, individuals and Federal Agencies are eligible to receive funding. No matching funds are required.

IV. Approach

To accomplish the objectives of this RFP, cores should be collected in estuarine and coastal areas, carefully dated and analyzed for trace metals and organic compounds.

For the first year, priority will be given to four estuaries and coastal areas: The Savannah Estuary, southern California Bight, San Francisco Bay and Puget Sound. Depending on the availability of funds, areas may be dropped.

We are interested in identifying contamination trends in sediments since the early 1900s and even since the early 1800s for the trace metals; therefore, the cores have to be undisturbed and collected in areas where sedimentation rates are sufficiently high to give a reliable dating for the last 100 years. The parameters to be measured are the trace elements and the organic chemicals routinely measured in the NS&T Program (appendix A: Table 1 and 2). In addition, nutrients such as N, P and C_{org} should be included. The level needed for

Figure 3-1. Sample federal register announcement.

spondence or other future references to this solicitation. A description of the proposed project or procurement is provided in a brief but detailed fashion, usually with sufficient facts to give the reader an idea of whether it might represent a possibility for his or her organization. This will include special factors such as a preference for small businesses or minority businesses, if applicable. The notice will also include an application deadline and often a phone number for obtaining more information.

Like the *Federal Register, Commerce Business Daily* may be obtained by mail from the U.S. Government Printing Office (Washington, D.C. 20402). The cost is $173 per year via nonpriority mail, and $243 yearly for priority mail. Electronic versions are available. An alternative to subscribing is to review copies available in public libraries, university libraries, Small Business Administration offices, or Department of Commerce field offices, among other locations.

Catalog of Federal Domestic Assistance

A different type of information is provided by the *Catalog of Federal Domestic Assistance* (CFDA). Unlike the *Federal Register* or *Commerce Business Daily,* this directory emphasizes ongoing programs rather than announcements of individual grant competitions. This makes it less timely but more useful if you are trying to get a broad picture of programs that might apply to your small business.

Say you are interested in developing a new strain of Christmas tree that stays green longer after it has been cut. Are grants and contracts available in this area? A quick check of the *Catalog of Federal Domestic Assistance* will reveal that yes, several possibilities might be worth examining. The index will lead you to an entry under "Agricultural Research Service, Department of Agriculture." Further examination will show specific individual programs such as program no. 10.001, Agricultural Research—Basic and Applied Research. (Each program has a special five-digit identification number so that it can be readily identified—a helpful practice considering the long, involved names given to many federal agencies and programs.) You can review that section to see if program 10.001 represents a potential funding source for your business. If so, the next step would be to write or call for information on the next cycle of grant applications and awards.

Privately Published Newsletters

The standard government publications are by no means the only information available. A number of companies publish directories, newsletters, or other materials which can be perused for details about grant and contract programs.

A good example is *Federal Grants and Contracts Weekly,* published by Capitol Publications (P.O. Box 1453, Alexandria, Virginia 22313-2053). This newsletter, usually 8 or 10 pages long, provides up-to-date information about available grants and contracts. Many details are taken from the *Federal Register* and *Commerce Business Daily,* although other sources are also used. As a result there is some duplication with government publications, but the information is more readable and efficiently presented and only material relevant to grants and contracts is retained. In essence, your subscription dollars are paying for the newsletter staff to peruse government information sources, saving you the time needed to do the same thing. In addition, you get updates on new legislation, changes in government regulations, and other potentially important details.

Each issue contains a "News Briefing" section, which provides background information, and a "Grants Alert" section, which lists upcoming grant competitions. This section includes the scope of each program involved, the application deadline, amount of funds available, who is eligible to apply, areas covered, and addresses and phone numbers where more information (including application packets) can be obtained. Another section, "RFP's Available," provides announcements of government contract competitions including deadlines, eligibility requirements, and where to obtain application materials.

Similar information is provided by several other newsletters. One of the better known is *Federal Research Report,* issued weekly. Published by Business Publishers Incorporated (951 Pershing Drive, Silver Spring, MD 20910-4464), this newsletter provides current information about various upcoming programs for which proposals may be submitted. A typical issue is eight pages long. This usually includes a general section on news and trends such as congressional hearings, new government policies, and promising program developments. Individual program announcements are then divided among categories such as health, education, energy, environment, defense, meetings and publications, social sciences, transportation, and miscellaneous. Each announcement includes basic information including a description of the program, the deadline date (printed in boldface type for easy identification), and where to obtain application materials or more information.

Like others of its type, *Federal Research Report* offers the advantages of timeliness and succinct presentation of information. It is easy to use and can save a great deal of time when compared to the longer, more detailed government publications.

Another publication in this vein is *Federal Assistance Monitor,* which is published twice monthly by CD Publications (8204 Fenton Street, Silver Spring, MD 20910). In addition to reports on grant and contract opportunities, if offers news about policy changes, program interpretations, and other useful background details. The *Monitor* also provides tips on proposal preparation, and for paid subscribers, the staff will critique one grant application at no charge.

The Grant Advisor (P.O. Box 520, Linden, VA 22642) also provides similar information. It is published 11 times a year and covers private foundation grants (virtually all of which go to nonprofit organizations or individuals) along with government programs. Short descriptions of grant programs and current competitions furnish a quick overview of each program, with emphasis placed on criteria for selection of grantees, eligibility, and anticipated funding levels. Special features include a roundup section called "Et Cetera"; a list of grant deadlines; and a supplement, "The Grant Advisor," covering various material such as how-to tips on different aspects of grant development. An interesting feature is that the entire publication is available on computer as an alternative to hard copy. Subscribers who opt for this method receive their issues on computer diskettes.

In deciding which publication is best for your needs, consider cost, frequency of issuance, relevance to the goals and products of your company, and competing sources of information. In some cases it may be advisable to subscribe to several sources, but it is easy to overdo this and end up paying for the same details more than once. Before making a commitment, request free examination copies and take a close look at samples. If your funds are tight, check with libraries in your area and see what is available.

Nonfederal Programs

The major emphasis of this book is on grant and contract programs offered by the federal government, but other possibilities exist. State and municipal governments, for example, may also hold grant or contract competitions. To find out about such programs, you will need to identify and use the information sources unique to your locality. This might include local or statewide newspapers, mailing lists, or other outlets.

Here are several approaches for finding out about grant or contract possibilities in your state or area:

1. Find out which state agency is responsible for purchasing or procurement of goods or services, and ask that your company's name be placed on any mailing lists that might include information about contract or grant competitions.

2. Do the same thing for other major agencies which might have a possible connection with the type of work performed by your company. Say you operate a small business which grows and harvests fish as a food source. Since aquaculture is a relatively new technology, your state may not have a department which oversees this per se but may spread the responsibility between two or more state agencies such as the Department of Agriculture (or its equivalent) and whatever department deals with fisheries in your state. To be safe, ask both agencies to place your name on any mailing lists dealing with grants or contracts. A simple form letter is all that is needed for this; see Fig. 3-2 for an example.

3. Check with the nearest small business center, and indicate your in-

(Your letterhead)
(date)

TO WHOM IT MAY CONCERN:

I am interested in learning of any possibilities for applying for grants or contracts for which small businesses are eligible to compete. Please forward any available information, and place my name on any mailing lists to receive RFP's or other information. Please send to the following address:

Timothy Smith
Smith Aquaculture
2200 Walden Road
White Falls, VA 24803

Thank you for your cooperation.

Sincerely,

Timothy E. Smith, Vice President

Figure 3-2. Sample letter for mailing list placement.

terest in possible grants and contracts. Ask if any information is available on grants and contracts for which small businesses might apply.

4. If you live in a large city, follow the same course of action with municipal officials.

5. Review classified sections of local or state newspapers, newsletters, bulletin boards in public buildings, and other publications for information about funding possibilities. Some states issue manuals or other publications which explain how to pursue procurement contracts or other awards; these can be particularly helpful.

6. If you have difficulty locating the appropriate information, check with your representative in the state legislature. He or she should be able to point you in the right direction to find the information you need.

Once you locate sources of funding, the proposal process will be similar to that followed for applications for federal funds. The approaches described in later chapters can be easily adapted to seeking funds at the state or local government level.

What to Look For

In any announcement soliciting proposals, there will be certain key points on which you should focus your attention. Reading even the briefest of newsletters takes time, a commodity few people operating small businesses can afford to waste. To keep your investment of time to a minimum, don't bother reading the whole entry about any program on a word-for-word basis. Instead, scan through the material and assess the following:

1. *Eligibility.* Requirements for eligibility may not be the first item listed, but for businesses it is the most important. Look for this heading (sometimes printed in boldface) and the important information which follows. Common eligibility categories include such designations as "nonprofit organizations," "institutions of higher education," "public and nonprofit agencies," "state agencies," "LEA's [local educational agencies]" and "nonprofit and for-profit organizations." The term "for-profit" is the key here; if only nonprofits are eligible, there is no need to read further. If the for-profit designation or similar language is used, further review might be warranted.

2. *Deadline.* Most programs have a specific date by which proposals must be submitted (some are open-ended and will accept proposals at any time, but these are in the minority). Some competitions are con-

ducted annually, some more often, and others are offered on a one-time basis only. At any rate, the next step after determining eligibility is to check the announced deadline and see how much time remains to complete an application. Obviously the greater the time available, the better, for you will need time to prepare an effective proposal. A lead time of a few weeks is typical, but you might have less. In this case it might not be practical to make the commitment of applying, unless you are good at crash projects or already have a similar proposal completed which could be reworked for submission to the new program. At any rate, a tentative "go" or "no go" decision at this point will rest at least in part on the deadline.

3. *Funding level or scope of work.* Most grant announcements will provide some idea of the anticipated funding level. This may be presented for the overall program (for example, a statement that a total of $500,000 is available), or such a figure combined with the anticipated number of grant awards (e.g., a total of $500,000 to be awarded, with six to eight projects expected to be funded). Or the announcement might stipulate a set amount per project (for example, an average grant award of $40,000) or a maximum amount per award (such as no grant to be awarded exceeding $35,000). Whatever the case, having an idea from the outset can help you determine if the program is worth pursuing. The potential funding range may seem too small to be worth the trouble, or at the other extreme so large that it would exceed the capacity of your particular small business to undertake.

Announcements about contracts will generally differ from those about grants, since the cost of the project may depend on what the applicant proposes and can be a major selection criterion. Instead, the description may estimate the time it will take to complete the defined tasks (for example, at least 10,000 worker-hours). As with a budget estimate for a grant, such information provides a quick idea of the scope any funded project would have.

4. *Where to obtain information.* Every announcement will include a telephone number for obtaining more information, a mailing address, or both. These details can be useful if you have questions about the program, but even more important, they tell you where to obtain application forms and deadlines. More about obtaining application materials will be covered below in this chapter.

5. *Program or solicitation numbers.* Most programs will have a number which can be used in any correspondence or related documentation. This might be a standard CFDA number (from the *Catalog of Federal Domestic Assistance*) or a solicitation number for onetime use in a grant or contract solicitation. Whatever the case, it is a good idea to use this

number in any letters or other correspondence, as well as in proposals. Names of programs can be quite similar and thus confusing, but the accompanying number will help prevent mistakes such as having the wrong application packet sent to you.

Obtaining Application Materials

Once you have identified a potential source of funding, the next step is to obtain application materials. This will usually include a booklet or kit with application forms, directions for completing them, and background information about the need being addressed and the program being sponsored.

The first question to ask yourself is whether to phone or write for this information. Some programs (especially contract competitions) will accept written requests only. Many program announcements, on the other hand, include both a mailing address and a telephone number. Facsimile numbers are not usually provided, and fax seems unlikely to be used extensively in the near future because of the expense agencies would undergo in transmitting information.

If a phone number is provided and the deadline seems uncomfortably close, it may be best to telephone and request materials. The advantage here is that you can save several days or more compared with the time a letter, and then its response, might require in transit. The disadvantages include the cost of a long-distance call and the possibility that the person who takes your call could forget to follow up promptly, or even at all. This latter problem should not happen, but it is a possibility, since there would be no written reminder such as a letter.

If time is not a particular problem, the best approach is to send a brief letter, or a postcard, requesting the information you need. This can be a form letter which does not need to look like originally produced correspondence, since the process at this point is purely clerical and there is no need to worry about appearances. Figure 3-3 shows a sample letter which you can use. It is important to include the name of the program, the program or solicitation number (if given), and your address.

Following Up

When you receive an application packet, you should have everything you need to begin the application process. A smart step at this point is to take some time and read through the packet to see if an application still

TRT Incorporated
Box 3346
Greenville, SC 29611
(Date)

Dear Program Officials:

Please send me application materials for the following:

____

____

____

Thank you for your cooperation.

Sincerely,
John H. Yourname,
President

(NOTE: Be sure to fill in any number which has been cited such as a solicitation number or federal program number, along with the name of the program or competition. To save time, it is acceptable to preprint blank copies of this letter and fill in the information with a pen or typewriter.)

Figure 3-3. Sample letter for requesting application materials.

seems to be worthwhile, since additional details will probably be provided which were not noted in the initial announcement.

If you are seriously interested in pursuing multiple opportunities, it may be helpful to record some basic information about each application packet you review. This can be used for future reference and may save you the trouble of requesting and reviewing material twice for the same program (this is more likely than it may seem due to the often complex nature of program names and descriptions). You might want to develop a simple form for this purpose. Figure 3-4 is an example.

If you still believe the opportunity looks promising, begin putting a proposal together. Chapter 4 covers the basic elements of a proposal, and Chap. 5 provides tips on making the most of your efforts to develop a competitive application. Your work may just be beginning, but you can do it—and a substantial grant or contract award may be the result!

SRR, Inc.
Funding Source Review Sheet

Name of Program/Agency:

Date of Review:

Eligibility:

______For-profit organizations clearly eligible
______For-profit organizations possibly eligible
______Small-business set-aside
______Businesses not eligible to apply

Comments:

Follow Up:

______Definitely apply
______Possibly apply
______Defer for future consideration or review
______File
______Discard application materials but retain this form

Figure 3-4. Sample form for recording information about funding sources.

4 Developing Proposals

Too often, advertisements for seminars and educational materials would have you believe that government funds are available in large sums just for the asking. They imply that if you just know where to look, thousands or millions of dollars will be given to you by simply making a phone call or filling out a few forms.

In most cases, this is far from the truth. Instead, the process is genuinely competitive. But that's okay! After all, you're a business, not a charity. If you're like most people in the small business sector, all you really want is a fair chance to compete. And that is what the federal government offers to those small businesses which are savvy and aggressive enough to go after government funding.

In a typical grant or contract program, this is the way it works: eligible organizations or individuals prepare written application forms which are then assessed by the funding agency, and those with the best proposals receive funding. *Best* in this context means those that most convincingly build a case that a need exists, or if the need has already been established, that they are best suited for addressing it.

For the small business, this amounts to building a convincing case similar to a sales proposal or other business proposal but with some additional elements. The written grant or contract proposal represents the applicant's statement of capability, interest, and particular needs or advantages. In short, it is an argument that your business is ready, able, and deserving to take on the project at hand.

To succeed in such efforts, you need first to understand what makes a good proposal and then put that knowledge into action. Every proposal contains certain key elements. Although formats vary, an under-

Table 4-1. Basic Proposal Elements

Cover sheet
Abstract
Table of contents
Background, need, or problem
Goals and objectives
Plan of operation, methodology, or implementation strategy
Evaluation strategy
Key personnel
Assurances
Appendixes

standing of basic proposal components will allow you to adapt to the situation at hand and develop applications which meet program requirements while competing successfully with other submissions.

Refer to Table 4-1 for the basic sections which make up many proposals for government funding. The remainder of this chapter discusses these elements in greater detail and provides tips for developing them.

In considering just what constitutes an effective proposal, it is important to be aware that formats often vary among different agencies and programs and between grant and contract applications. Many contract proposals, for example, require two separate proposals: a technical proposal and a business proposal. Most grant applications, on the other hand, consist of a single, unified proposal. The information which follows is intended to provide a general overview of the types of elements most often encountered in proposals. Of course, you would adapt this information to the particular requirements spelled out in your RFP or application guidelines. You may wish to refer to a sample proposal that appears at the end of this chapter (Fig. 4-9) and a sample RFP included in App. D.

Cover Sheet

Most proposals include some type of cover sheet. Often, this is a preprinted form which must be filled in with a typewriter (computers and printers may be ineffective with such forms because of spacing restrictions). Different government agencies use different forms, but most will ask for some or all of the following details:

1. Type of submission (for example, preapplication, application, or notice of intent)
2. Applicant's self-assigned identifying number, if used
3. Legal name of applicant (such as, the name of your firm)
4. Applicant's address and telephone number
5. Name, title, and telephone number of project director or contact person
6. Employer identification number
7. Name and identifying number of the government program from which funds are being requested
8. Title of proposed project
9. Type of applicant (such as, nonprofit organization, business, individual)
10. Area of project impact (geographical area)
11. Type of assistance (grant, loan, etc.)
12. Proposed amount of funding
13. Congressional district of the applicant
14. Type or status of application (new or continuation)
15. Date project would begin, if funded
16. Proposed project duration
17. Name of agency to which proposal is being submitted
18. Existing federal grant identification number (if applicable)
19. Name and title of individual authorized to commit applicant to the project
20. Signature of chief executive or other authorizing official

While this may seem to be a great deal of information, many of the details become routine responses once an initial proposal has been submitted and can be easily transferred from one proposal's cover sheet to another. For example, initially you may need to look up such details as employer identification number or applicant's congressional district, but then you can copy these into future proposals as needed.

Cover sheets may vary among government agencies. Figure 4-1 is an actual cover sheet for a U.S. Department of Education grant proposal. A similar document for a proposal to the National Science Foundation appears in Fig. 4-2.

OMB Approval No. 0348-0043

APPLICATION FOR FEDERAL ASSISTANCE

1. TYPE OF SUBMISSION: *Application* ☐ Construction ☐ Non-Construction; *Preapplication* ☐ Construction ☐ Non-Construction	2. DATE SUBMITTED	Applicant Identifier
	3. DATE RECEIVED BY STATE	State Application Identifier
	4. DATE RECEIVED BY FEDERAL AGENCY	Federal Identifier

5. APPLICANT INFORMATION

Legal Name:	Organizational Unit:
Address *(give city, county, state, and zip code)*:	Name and telephone number of the person to be contacted on matters involving this application *(give area code)*

6. EMPLOYER IDENTIFICATION NUMBER (EIN): ☐☐ – ☐☐☐☐☐☐☐

7. TYPE OF APPLICANT: *(enter appropriate letter in box)* ☐

A. State
B. County
C. Municipal
D. Township
E. Interstate
F. Intermunicipal
G. Special District
H. Independent School Dist.
I. State Controlled Institution of Higher Learning
J. Private University
K. Indian Tribe
L. Individual
M. Profit Organization
N. Other (Specify): ____________

8. TYPE OF APPLICATION:

☒ New ☐ Continuation ☐ Revision

If Revision, enter appropriate letter(s) in box(es): ☐ ☐

A. Increase Award B. Decrease Award C. Increase Duration
D. Decrease Duration Other *(specify)*:

____

9. NAME OF FEDERAL AGENCY:

10. CATALOG OF FEDERAL DOMESTIC ASSISTANCE NUMBER: ☐☐ - ☐☐☐

TITLE:

11. DESCRIPTIVE TITLE OF APPLICANT'S PROJECT:

12. AREAS AFFECTED BY PROJECT *(cities, counties, states, etc.)*:

13. PROPOSED PROJECT:		14. CONGRESSIONAL DISTRICTS OF:	
Start Date	Ending Date	a. Applicant	b. Project

15. ESTIMATED FUNDING:		
a. Federal	$	.00
b. Applicant	$	.00
c. State	$	.00
d. Local	$	.00
e. Other	$	.00
f. Program Income	$	.00
g. TOTAL	$	.00

16. IS APPLICATION SUBJECT TO REVIEW BY STATE EXECUTIVE ORDER 12372 PROCESS?

a. YES. THIS PREAPPLICATION/APPLICATION WAS MADE AVAILABLE TO THE STATE EXECUTIVE ORDER 12372 PROCESS FOR REVIEW ON:

DATE ____________

b. NO. ☐ PROGRAM IS NOT COVERED BY E.O. 12372

☐ OR PROGRAM HAS NOT BEEN SELECTED BY STATE FOR REVIEW

17. IS THE APPLICANT DELINQUENT ON ANY FEDERAL DEBT?

☐ Yes If "Yes," attach an explanation. ☐ No

18. TO THE BEST OF MY KNOWLEDGE AND BELIEF, ALL DATA IN THIS APPLICATION/PREAPPLICATION ARE TRUE AND CORRECT, THE DOCUMENT HAS BEEN DULY AUTHORIZED BY THE GOVERNING BODY OF THE APPLICANT AND THE APPLICANT WILL COMPLY WITH THE ATTACHED ASSURANCES IF THE ASSISTANCE IS AWARDED

a. Typed Name of Authorized Representative	b. Title	c. Telephone number
d. Signature of Authorized Representative		e. Date Signed

Previous Editions Not Usable

Standard Form 424 (REV 4-88)
Prescribed by OMB Circular A-102

Authorized for Local Reproduction

Figure 4-1. Sample cover sheet, U.S. Department of Education.

COVER SHEET FOR PROPOSALS TO THE NATIONAL SCIENCE FOUNDATION

FOR CONSIDERATION BY NSF ORGANIZATIONAL UNIT (Indicate the most specific unit known, i.e. program, division, etc	PROGRAM ANNOUNCEMENT/SOLICITATION NO./CLOSING DATE NSF 90-101 November 16, 1990
SUBMITTING INSTITUTION CODE (if known)	IS THIS PROPOSAL BEING SUBMITTED TO ANOTHER FEDERAL AGENCY? Yes___ No___ IF YES, LIST ACRONYM(S)

NAME OF SUBMITTING ORGANIZATION TO WHICH AWARD SHOULD BE MADE (INCLUDE BRANCH/CAMPUS/OTHER COMPONENTS)

ADDRESS OF ORGANIZATION (INCLUDE ZIP CODE)

IS SUBMITTING ORGANIZATION: ☐ For-Profit Organization; ☐ Small Business; ☐ Minority Business; ☐ Woman-Owned Business

TITLE OF PROPOSED PROJECT

REQUESTED AMOUNT (a)	Non-NSF Contribution (b)	Total Project Cost (a + b)

CHECK APPROPRIATE BOX(ES) IF THIS PROPOSAL INCLUDES ANY OF THE ITEMS LISTED BELOW:

☐ Animal Welfare	☐ National Environmental Policy Act	☐ International Cooperative Activity
☐ Endangered Species	☐ Research Involving Recombinant DNA Molecules	☐ Research Opportunity Award
☐ Human Subjects		☐ Facilitation Award for Handicapped
☐ Marine Mammal Protection	☐ Historical Sites	☐ Proprietary and Privileged Information
☐ Pollution Control	☐ Interdisciplinary	

PI/PD DEPARTMENT	PI/PD ORGANIZATION	PI/PD PHONE NO. & ELECTRONIC MAIL

PI/PD NAME/TITLE	SOCIAL SECURITY NO.*	HIGHEST DEGREE & YEAR	SIGNATURE
ADDITIONAL PI/PD (TYPED)			
ADDITIONAL PI/PD (TYPED)			
ADDITIONAL PI/PD (TYPED)			
ADDITIONAL PI/PD (TYPED)			

For NSF Use:

TO BE COMPLETED BY THE AUTHORIZED ORGANIZATIONAL REPRESENTATIVE. By signing and submitting this proposal, the prospective grantee is providing the certifications set forth in (1) *Grants for Research and Education in Science and Engineering*, NSF 83-57 (rev. 11/87), and (2) Appendix C, 45CFR 620, Subpart F (Requirements for a Drug-Free Workplace).

(If answering *yes* to either, please provide explanation.)	YES	NO
Is the organization delinquent on any Federal Debt?		
Is the organization presently debarred, suspended, proposed for debarment, declared ineligible, or voluntarily excluded from covered transactions by any Federal department or agency?		

AUTHORIZED ORGANIZATIONAL REP.	SIGNATURE	DATE	TELEPHONE NO.
NAME/TITLE (TYPED)			
OTHER ENDORSEMENT (optional)			
NAME/TITLE (TYPED)			

*Submission of social security numbers is voluntary and will not affect the organization's eligibility for an award. However, they are an integral part of the NSF information system and assist in processing the proposal. SSN solicited under NSF Act of 1950, as amended.

Figure 4-2. Sample cover sheet, National Science Foundation.

In some competitions, a standard cover form may not be provided. In that case, a simple cover sheet can be devised listing a few basic details such as name of the applicant, the title or subject of the proposal, and any other details you may want to provide.

Abstract

An abstract is a very brief summary of the proposal. As a minimum, it should include the following elements, stated as succinctly as possible:

1. The problem being addressed
2. The activities proposed
3. The intended outcomes of the project

If an abstract is required, the application guidelines will probably provide specific guidelines about length and format. For example, the abstract may be limited to one double-spaced page. Or it might be measured by the word, such as a 250- or 400-word maximum.

In some instances, a form will be provided for the abstract. In others, you can simply use an ordinary sheet of paper.

Abstracts can be used in several different ways and may be more important than they might initially appear. Government staff members and external reviewers may read the abstract first to obtain a quick overview of the proposal. The old adage "first impressions count" often holds true, and a well-written abstract can help make a positive impression on the reader. In addition, abstracts are often used in government reports when it is not possible to provide a long, detailed description of the project. These reports may be distributed widely, in the process representing your project (and your business) to readers who know nothing else about it. As a result, it is in your best interest to develop a clear, well-organized abstract.

You can follow one of two approaches in writing the abstract. One is to develop the abstract (or at least a rough draft) before writing the rest of the proposal. This procedure can help you formulate the basic approach while developing key concepts such as the project methodology and the outcomes intended. It can also provide a useful document for sharing your ideas with others at the preproposal stage.

An alternative method is to wait until the proposal has been completed and only then write the abstract. An advantage here is that you will avoid wasting work if the direction of the proposal changes during development of the narrative or other portions of the application. In most cases completing the abstract is easier as one of the final steps because you have already presented the basic information needed and need only restate it in abbreviated form.

In either case, observing the following tips should make the abstract as effective as possible:

1. Be sure to observe length limitations. If a certain number of words is specified, check the word count carefully. Computer spell-checking programs, which usually provide a word count at the end of the spell-checking process, can come in handy here.

2. Use short, simple sentences. Short is the key rule in any abstract. If a sentence seems too long (say more than 20 words), break it into two shorter ones. Also, avoid frequent use of adjectives and adverbs.

3. Write a rough draft and then edit it. Editing a rough draft and deleting unnecessary words is usually easier than trying to get every word just right during the first draft.

4. Don't overemphasize the need for the project. A sentence or two about the need for a project may be desirable, but the abstract is not the place to build your case as to why funds are needed. Instead, the abstract should focus on other factors such as what will be done and what results are anticipated.

5. Don't dwell on the budget. The budget information will be provided elsewhere. Don't waste precious space addressing it in the abstract.

6. Take time to review the finished abstract. Be sure to read the material for clarity and completeness, and then add any fine points which may be needed.

A sample abstract for a project by the U.S. Department of Education appears in Fig. 4-3.

Table of Contents

For longer proposals, a table of contents may be helpful (and in some cases, required). This should list each major section of the proposal and include the page numbers where each section begins.

A good organizational pattern is to include an entry for each criterion area against which the proposal will be evaluated. For instance, simply listing "narrative" is not sufficient; separate headings or subheadings should also be included for each section of the narrative such as need or

DEPARTMENT OF EDUCATION
RFP NUMBER 90-010

TOPIC NUMBER 3
DEVELOPMENT OF MANAGEMENT INFORMATION SYSTEM SOFTWARE CONCERNED WITH THE NEEDS OF INDIVIDUALS WITH DISABILITIES AND THEIR FAMILIES

A MULTI-PLATFORM COMPUTER-ASSISTED INDIVIDUAL FAMILY SERVICE PLAN FOR EARLY INTERVENTION PROGRAMS

COMPANY: EduCom, Inc.
21 Salt Island Road
Gloucester, MA 01930

PRINCIPAL INVESTIGATOR: Paul J. Jackson
President, EduCom, Inc.
21 Salt Island Road
Gloucester, MA 01930

ABSTRACT: This project is designed to develop a computer-assisted method of developing the Individual Family Service Plan (IFSP) required of Early Intervention programs as part of the 1986 Education of the Handicapped Act.

Because of the constantly changing developmental phases of the birth to five year old population, specific long term achievements are very difficult for professionals to predict. As a result, hand-written IFSP's must be constantly modified to reflect child growth and new developmental goals - a significant administrative burden for professional staff, a significant expense for administrative staff and a confusing process for families.. A computer system that allows the therapist and teachers to monitor growth and plan for achievement in an efficient and effective manner is necessary to maintain the quality of service for a constantly increasing population.

This project will develop an IFSP system that will: 1) provide basic administrative data on each child; 2) accurately describe skills, abilities and needs of the child and family 3) outline near-term goals and objectives for the child and family; 4) monitor the outlined goals, noting achievement, adding new goals, and modifying goals based upon the child's growth; 5) provide child and family with clear and understandable IFSP's and progress reports.

KEYWORDS: Early Intervention, IFSP, Goal, Objectives, database

ANTICIPATED RESULTS: Phase I will result in the completion of a Needs Assessment specifically focused on how the IFSP is developed at Early Intervention sites, the contents of the IFSP, and the goals that program staff, directors, and State Part H coordinators have for the IFSP form. Based upon that information, a prototype IFSP form will be developed and programmed on an MS-DOS computer

Phase II will result in the development of a complete IFSP System on an MS-DOS, Apple II and Macintosh computer. All platforms will be identical in operation. An integral part of the system will be the development of a library of goals and objectives specifically targeted to the needs of Early Intervention programs.

COMMERCIAL APPLICATION: The IFSP development program that will be developed will be, with minor revision, applicable to all programs that write plans for individual achievement: mental health agencies, special education, drug and alcohol rehabilitation services are just a few of the potential clients.

Figure 4-3. Sample abstract.

problem statement, goals, specific objectives, evaluation strategies, and so forth.

For proposals of fewer than 10 pages, a table of contents may be unnecessary. If in doubt, consult directions for completing the application, and in the case of short proposals, include a contents page only if stipulated.

Project Narrative

The project narrative may contain several components. It is usually the longest single portion of a proposal. Here, the applicant explains the basic concept behind the proposal and builds a case for funding.

Following is an overview of various components which might be included in the narrative.

Background, Introduction, or Mission

If you are applying as a business rather than as an individual, it may be appropriate to provide a background statement about your company. If the competition for which you are applying is also open to nonprofit organizations, this section will be where such applicants describe their mission and purpose. In one sense, these matters may not seem relevant to businesses. But a short statement describing your firm may be in order, if for no other reason than to avoid suffering in comparison to nonprofit applicants or the appearance of not responding to one of the major categories of the narrative.

In describing any for-profit enterprise, it is wise to emphasize an overall purpose aside from generating profits. The profit motive need not be hidden, for readers will understand that any business is interested in this angle. But an overriding purpose, such as "to develop alternative methods for providing economical home heating and cooling" or "to provide computer support services for new and emerging organizations" will help provide readers with a basic understanding of your company. Additional details might include how long your company has existed, major initiatives or unusual features, and similar information.

Need or Problem Statement

A statement of the need being addressed is a standard element of many proposals. This is true more often in grant proposals than in contracts, for the latter generally address a specific need which has already been identified by the funding source (that is, for most contracts you do not need to "sell" the government on the idea that your project is necessary but only that your firm is best suited to carry out the work described in the request for proposals).

With most grant proposals, however, part of your task is to convince readers that a genuine need exists for the project you are proposing. This may be based on local, state, or national needs, or even in some cases on needs within your own organization. For example, a proposal to the Department of Agriculture may be based on your belief that it is necessary to develop a hardier strain of beets so that they can be grown in areas of the country where weather conditions are presently deemed unsatisfactory for beets. In making such an assertion, you might point to specific problems in this area (such as lack of beet production, instances of failed attempts to grow beets in certain geographical areas, a government report indicating the need to increase production of sugar from beets, and so forth). Or say you are submitting a proposal to the Department of Labor to conduct a special training program providing job skills to unemployed adults. To enhance the chance of obtaining funding, you will need to demonstrate that a significant number of adults in your area actually need the training you propose. This might be supported by citing unemployment figures, describing industry cutbacks or plant closings, or summarizing a study of employment and training needs in your region.

The key element in a need statement is sufficient information to convince readers that a significant problem exists which could be positively addressed if funding were provided. In other words, is the problem you are discussing really important? And if so, would government support for addressing the problem represent a worthwhile use of public funds? If the answer to both questions is an obvious yes, any chances of receiving funding will be strengthened.

An effective need or problem statement should:

1. *Make a clear statement of need.* The reader should not have to guess what need is being addressed and the stance the writer is taking toward it. Is some corrective action necessary? If so, this should be made clear early in the proposal.

2. *Back up assertions with facts or figures.* Just saying that a need exists is not enough. It is important to provide some evidence to support your assertion. Pertinent statistics, quotations from reputable publications, or research citations can be effective here.

3. *Avoid hyperbole.* Overstating the case can harm a proposal more than help it. It is necessary only to establish that a need exists, not assert that it is the most pressing problem in Western civilization.

4. *Mesh with other sections of the proposal.* The need statement should be completely consistent with other elements of the application. Ideally, it should set the stage by describing problems in such a way that the implementation strategies which follow seem the best possible solution.

Goals and Objectives

Once you have established that a need exists for a given activity, the next step is to state the goals and objectives for the proposed project. Writing goals and objectives is one of the most important aspects of proposal development. It requires precise wording and careful organization.

The words *goal* and *objective* are too often used interchangeably, but they actually have different meanings. A *goal* is a general statement of a desired change. This statement does not necessarily need to be measurable. A commonly cited example is the goal of losing weight. This can be a general plan or desire without specifying an amount of weight to be lost, a time frame to achieve the loss, or other similar details.

An *objective,* on the other hand, should be more specific. It should indicate not just the change that is desired but also the degree of change anticipated, ideally in measurable terms. An example would be to lose 25 lb in eight weeks as opposed to the general goal of simply losing weight.

Ideally, goals and objectives should be developed together, with objectives growing out of goal statements. Each goal should have at least one specific objective that is directly related to that goal. Goals and objectives should both be based on the problems which have been discussed in the need statement or introductory material.

Goal statements should be:

1. Clearly identified as goals (for example, they may be identified with a lead-in statement such as "the goals of the proposed project are as follows," followed by a colon and the goal statements themselves)
2. Succinctly stated
3. Reasonable (limited to tasks that can be accomplished within normal expectations of workloads, technical limitations, and other parameters)

4. Consistent with funding agency priorities (only those goals directly related to the priorities of the funding agency or a particular program should be included)

Objectives should be:

1. Related directly to goals (each objective should support a goal statement)
2. More specific than goals
3. Concisely stated
4. Measurable, if possible (worded in such a way that the degree to which they are accomplished can be assessed)
5. Based on identified needs
6. Ambitious without being unrealistic (challenging but achievable within the time for which project funding is requested)

It is vital that goals and objectives be thought through carefully and written with great care. A subpar job of writing goals and objectives can not only cause reviewers to subtract rating points in their assessment of the proposal but also weaken other portions of the application, since the implementation plan and other elements are based heavily on goals and objectives. In most cases, objectives become mechanisms for measuring the project's success if you receive funding. They are like promises which must be met later and thus should be formulated with care. Following are some examples of effectively constructed statements for goals and objectives:

Goal. To improve job-finding capabilities of local residents who are unemployed or underemployed.

Objective. To provide specialized job training for at least seventy-five (75) people aged 18–30 over a six-month period.

Goal. To meet job Training Partnership Act eligibility standards.

Objective. To see that one hundred (100) percent of all clients served by this program meet JTPA guidelines for eligibility.

Goal. To develop an alternative mechanism for measuring toxic emissions from abandoned coal mines.

Objective. To field-test at least two (2) new devices for measurement of emissions of toxic substances from coal mines by the end of the first project year.

Goal. To involve more minority clients in specialized job counseling.

Objective. To increase by fifteen (15) percent the number of minority clients served over the number served during the previous 12 months.

Goal statements are not always required, but even so it is helpful to develop them before writing objectives. That way, you will be more likely to develop objectives which are specific and measurable, in contrast to the generalities making up goal statements.

If you provide both goals and objectives, they need not always have a one-for-one relationship. A single goal can lead to any number of objectives. On the other hand, every goal to be addressed in a project should generate at least one specific objective.

In many applications for contracts and in some other proposals, it is not necessary to develop either goals or objectives. These may already have been identified by government staffers, and your task is simply to show how you intend to meet these preestablished targets. The terms *goals* and *objectives* may not even be used; instead, RFPs and proposals may refer to such terms as "functions," "tasks," and "subtasks." The applicant may not have to write these but simply agree to conduct them.

Plan of Operation

No section of a proposal is more important than the plan of operation. This is the part of the proposal which explains how the goals and objectives will be carried out. It is here that readers learn just what you plan to do if the project is funded.

This section may be called the "methodology," "implementation plan," "implementation strategy," or a similar term. In many applications it is the longest and most detailed portion of the narrative.

As a minimum, the plan of operation should describe all activities which will be conducted and also specify when they will be completed. It may also explain various other details depending on application instructions for format and content, as well as your own preferences.

A typical plan of operation or methodology will include some or all of the following:

1. *Overall description of strategies.* What work will be accomplished through this project? Will there be research conducted? A product produced? Training conducted? A detailed narrative description should cover such points.
2. *Background information.* How were the strategies developed?

Were other alternatives considered? Why are these particular steps a good idea? What information has been used in the development of these strategies?

3. *Implementation timetable.* What milestones have been established for carrying out project activities? When will the project begin? When will each major step take place? When will the project conclude? Such details may be described in narrative form or may be built into a table or both.

4. *Data collection.* If data will be collected, how will the information be gathered? What controls have been established? How will the data be reported and used?

5. *Innovative aspects.* Does the proposed project have any innovative features? If so, how will the proposed innovation represent an improvement over existing practices? Why do you believe the methods chosen are likely to be effective?

6. *Potential impact.* What impact will the project have if successfully completed? What outcomes do you anticipate? Will the impact be of local scope, or will it have regional or national significance?

Depending on the type of proposal and the requirements which have been established for any particular competition, this section can be quite long and complicated. It might be 5 pages long in one proposal or over 100 pages in another. The application instructions will often provide details on the preferred length and will almost always list key points which should be covered. If this is not clear, refer to the portion of the instructions which lists "evaluation criteria," and then make certain that each criterion listed is addressed fully in the project narrative.

In developing the project narrative, be sure to do the following:

- *Don't skimp on information.* If a maximum length of 20 pages is mandated, a 6- or 8-page narrative probably will not include enough information. In most cases, you should fill most or all of the allowable space.
- *Follow application instructions carefully.* Make sure that each point mentioned in the guidelines is addressed somewhere in the narrative.
- *Explain details as fully as possible.* Don't assume readers will automatically understand every statement you make. Define terms, back up assertions, and explain the thought process behind major premises. Also, explain information which may be widely known locally but perhaps not elsewhere. For example, perhaps your firm is located in a rural area with a large population of Native Americans. Readers

in Washington, DC, may not realize this unless you make a point of it. Yet if your project is service- or education-oriented, this might make a difference in how it is perceived.

- *Develop an air of competence.* Throughout the project narrative, try to sound well-informed and competent. By citing recognized authorities on a given subject, for example, you come across as having done your homework. You sound authoritative, even if you and your firm are relatively inexperienced.

Evaluation Plan

How will you evaluate the activities of the project to determine their effectiveness? This is an important question which must be addressed in most proposals. Government representatives tend to be particularly interested in this matter, for it is through such measures that project accountability is maintained. Proposal reviewers are usually asked to rate this section with a specific point total, and will deduct points for a weak evaluation component. Thus a poorly designed evaluation section alone can keep you from getting an award.

In addition, if your project is lucky enough to receive funding, you need an effective evaluation component so that you know exactly what effects the project *is having* while it is ongoing (a formative evaluation) and what effects it *has had* after the project or an activity within the project has concluded (a summative evaluation). Not only is this useful for anyone connected with the project but also the evaluation results can be key to obtaining further funding.

The main element of evaluation is identifying changes (hopefully positive ones) from the way things stand *before* project activities took place to the way they are *after* they have been undertaken. Usually this involves collecting some kind of "baseline" data for use in making such comparisons, as well as gathering comparison data at other points of development.

The U.S. Department of Education recommends the following measures in designing project evaluation:

- Construct clear and measurable objectives that have measurable qualities
- Select measures that specify who, when, and how the data will be collected, analyzed, and reported
- Build evaluation measures into the routines of program measures, rather than appending them

- Use multiple measures, rather than a single measure, when possible
- Orient evaluation measures primarily toward behavior (where applicable)
- Employ established measures, rather than locally created ones, when feasible
- Use program documents and records for ongoing process evaluation
- Consult evaluation experts about the project's evaluation design
- Collect information on the program's cost-effectiveness

Evaluation may seem a complicated process, but the design of an effective evaluation can be accomplished by anyone who is willing to master basic evaluation principles. To learn more about the subject, consult a work such as *Thinking about Program Evaluation,* by Richard Berk and Peter Rossi (Sage, Beverly Hills, 1990), or *Program Evaluation: A Field Guide for Administrators,* by Robert Schalock and Craig Thornton (Plenum, New York, 1988). Such books can be obtained in local libraries or academic libraries, requested through interlibrary loan if not available locally, or purchased in bookstores.

Once you develop evaluation strategies for one proposal, the same principles may be reused or adapted in other proposals. You can also consult agency staff members during the preproposal stage for advice in this area, in some cases.

Key Personnel

Most applications will also include a section on key personnel who will be involved in the project. This is a very important item, for it shows reviewers that your firm is competent to take on the project being proposed.

As a minimum, the following information should be provided:

1. A description of the project director's capabilities for carrying out the project
2. An indication of the percentage of time the project director will spend in directing the project (for example, 10 percent, half-time, or full-time)
3. A description of the capabilities of other key staff members who will be involved in the project
4. An indication of the amount of time other staff members will spend on the project

In addition to this information, other details may be added here or in a section describing project management. This information can include a description of reporting arrangements, hiring policies, position descriptions, and résumés.

Position Descriptions

For each position to be funded through the project, it may be desirable to include a one-page job description. This is especially important for any position which will be added with project funds and for which an individual has not yet been identified. In some cases, position descriptions may be included with the project narrative, while in others, they may be added as appendixes. (Check application instructions for the preferred placement.)

A job description may include the following:

1. A listing of duties to be performed
2. The position supervising this position
3. Minimum qualifications for the job
4. The percentage of time devoted to each major duty.

Nondiscriminatory Practices

It is always a good idea to include a statement that your firm will engage in non-descriminatory practices in hiring and related matters. Even though this may be covered in assurance forms (discussed later), it is wise to include a statement to this effect in the section of the project narrative dealing with personnel. It is best not only to make a positive statement here but also to explain how your firm makes sure under-represented groups are encouraged to apply for position openings. Such groups should include most or all of the following:

- Racial minorities
- Women
- Handicapped people
- Older people

Résumés

A résumé or curriculum vitae may be required for personnel who will be associated with the project. Résumés are especially important for research projects where scientific or research credentials are necessary, but they may also be needed in other types of proposals. Instructions tend to vary rather widely regarding length, format, and other features for résumés. In some proposals, they will be limited to just one or two pages, while in others, longer résumés may be allowed.

Résumés should be up to date, neat, and informative. The overriding goal is to show competence for completing the work described in the proposal.

Résumé contents should include information such as the following:

- *Education.* List all educational institutions you have attended beginning with the postsecondary level, preferably in reverse chronological order. List names of institutions, locations, dates attended, degrees earned, and fields of specialization. To avoid confusion, do not use abbreviations (for example, USC may be interpreted as the University of Southern California by most readers, but some may think it refers to the University of South Carolina). You might also include seminars and short courses if they seem relevant to the topic of the proposal.
- *Work Experience.* List jobs you have held, beginning with the present and working backward. Include job title, employer, dates employed, and any special information not restricted by length limitations such as accomplishments or major tasks completed. Include military service if applicable.
- *Publications or Research Areas.* If you have had research or other work published, be sure to list it. Include a full citation which includes the name of the publication and the date it appeared. (This is more important in research proposals than in most others.)
- *Special Skills.* Try to think of any aspects of your background or skills which might apply to the proposed project, and list them here. For example, if you have been a manager for a large company but now are running your own business, you might list competencies in such areas as personnel supervision or inventory control. Or you might list familiarity with certain computer systems or other types of equipment.
- *Other Information.* Other details may be added as you see fit. Such items as hobbies, memberships in civic clubs, and future goals should be omitted, however.

Considering Your Own Qualifications

It is important to look objectively at your own qualifications or those of others in your firm when developing proposals. Will they make a positive impression on reviewers? This does not necessarily mean you must have a string of fancy degrees after your name—but if you do not, what other strengths can you list? Be sure to include any related accomplishments or experiences, and present information in such a way that you or your staff members appear ideally suited to conduct the planned activities.

In some cases, you can "buy" qualifications not possessed by employees of your company. In other words, you can propose to hire staff members or consultants with project funds who will carry out specialized activities. In this case, you will need to describe the proposed activities and explain that this is the way in which they will be completed. At the same time, you will still need to demonstrate competence for overseeing the project as proposed.

Budget

Every proposal will include a budget. Here you outline how much money you are requesting and how you propose to spend it.

For most grants, the idea or need is the main focus of the proposal, and this is the basis on which decisions are made as to whether the proposal is funded. The budget is seen as the means to an end in that the funds outlined represent the mechanism for achieving the goals and objectives proposed.

In some contract proposals, the budget is not so much a request for funds as a proposal to do the project for a certain amount of money. Some contract proposals are awarded first on the basis of technical merit, and then on the basis of cost; in other instances, particularly procurement contracts, the lowest bidder who is competent wins the award.

Budget development is a vital part of developing competitive proposals. More information on this facet of proposal development is covered in later chapters.

Assurances

When you apply for (or accept) government funds, you must agree to follow certain policies or practices. These include:

1. Nondiscrimination in hiring
2. Assurance that you will maintain a drug-free workplace
3. Compliance with a variety of personnel regulations
4. Compliance with other regulations specified by individual agencies

or programs (for example, environmental-impact limitations or protection of human subjects in research projects)

In addition, you must certify that your company has not been disbarred or otherwise made ineligible to receive federal funds.

To make these assurances, you must complete forms included in the application packet, date them, and provide signatures of the firm's chief executive officer. These forms should be read carefully before you sign them, but once that has been accomplished, the same information can be copied onto subsequent forms to accompany later proposals.

Figure 4-4 is a sample certification form relating to several government regulations. A certification promising to maintain a drug-free workplace is provided in Fig. 4-5. Figures 4-6 and 4-7 are assurances that your company has not been ruled ineligible to receive federal funds due to criminal activity or other problems or that you do not owe money to the government. Figure 4-8 is a form relating to lobbying activities.

It is important to avoid overlooking such forms during the proposal development process. A failure to include required forms can keep you from receiving an award or slow down the process of making an award if your proposal is selected for funding.

Appendixes

An *appendix* is an addition to a proposal. Appendixes can often prove useful if handled correctly. Reasons for adding one or more appendixes can include the following:

1. *To add material which would not fit logically within other sections of the proposal.* For example, letters of support may be included from organizations or individuals attesting to the need for the proposed program, capabilities of the applicant, and so forth. Or material which is too lengthy to fit in the narrative (such as an evaluation report from a previous year or tables of technical information) may fit more appropriately within an appendix.

2. *To circumvent length requirements.* When applications have specific maximum limits on the length of the narrative, it is sometimes worthwhile to include extra material in an appendix. It can be frustrating to have a maximum limit of 3 or 4 or even 20 pages for a narrative and then run out of room before providing all the information you would like. By adding such material in an appendix, there is at least a chance that reviewers will see the extra details and be positively influenced by them.

OMB Approval No. 0348-0040

ASSURANCES — NON-CONSTRUCTION PROGRAMS

Note: Certain of these assurances may not be applicable to your project or program. If you have questions, please contact the awarding agency. Further, certain Federal awarding agencies may require applicants to certify to additional assurances. If such is the case, you will be notified.

As the duly authorized representative of the applicant I certify that the applicant:

1. Has the legal authority to apply for Federal assistance, and the institutional, managerial and financial capability (including funds sufficient to pay the non-Federal share of project costs) to ensure proper planning, management and completion of the project described in this application.
2. Will give the awarding agency, the Comptroller General of the United States, and if appropriate, the State, through any authorized representative, access to and the right to examine all records, books, papers, or documents related to the award; and will establish a proper accounting system in accordance with generally accepted accounting standards or agency directives.
3. Will establish safeguards to prohibit employees from using their positions for a purpose that constitutes or presents the appearance of personal or organizational conflict of interest, or personal gain.
4. Will initiate and complete the work within the applicable time frame after receipt of approval of the awarding agency.
5. Will comply with the Intergovernmental Personnel Act of 1970 (42 U.S.C. §§ 4728-4763) relating to prescribed standards for merit systems for programs funded under one of the nineteen statutes or regulations specified in Appendix A of OPM's Standards for a Merit System of Personnel Administration (5 C.F.R. 900, Subpart F).
6. Will comply with all Federal statutes relating to nondiscrimination. These include but are not limited to: (a) Title VI of the Civil Rights Act of 1964 (P.L. 88-352) which prohibits discrimination on the basis of race, color or national origin; (b) Title IX of the Education Amendments of 1972, as amended (20 U.S.C. §§ 1681-1683, and 1685-1686), which prohibits discrimination on the basis of sex; (c) Section 504 of the Rehabilitation Act of 1973, as amended (29 U.S.C. § 794), which prohibits discrimination on the basis of handicaps; (d) the Age Discrimination Act of 1975, as amended (42 U.S.C. §§ 6101-6107), which prohibits discrimination on the basis of age; (e) the Drug Abuse Office and Treatment Act of 1972 (P.L. 92-255), as amended, relating to nondiscrimination on the basis of drug abuse; (f) the Comprehensive Alcohol Abuse and Alcoholism Prevention, Treatment and Rehabilitation Act of 1970 (P.L. 91-616), as amended, relating to nondiscrimination on the basis of alcohol abuse or alcoholism; (g) §§ 523 and 527 of the Public Health Service Act of 1912 (42 U.S.C. 290 dd-3 and 290 ee-3), as amended, relating to confidentiality of alcohol and drug abuse patient records; (h) Title VIII of the Civil Rights Act of 1968 (42 U.S.C. § 3601 et seq.), as amended, relating to nondiscrimination in the sale, rental or financing of housing; (i) any other nondiscrimination provisions in the specific statute(s) under which application for Federal assistance is being made; and (j) the requirements of any other nondiscrimination statute(s) which may apply to the application.
7. Will comply, or has already complied, with the requirements of Titles II and III of the Uniform Relocation Assistance and Real Property Acquisition Policies Act of 1970 (P.L. 91-646) which provide for fair and equitable treatment of persons displaced or whose property is acquired as a result of Federal or federally assisted programs. These requirements apply to all interests in real property acquired for project purposes regardless of Federal participation in purchases.
8. Will comply with the provisions of the Hatch Act (5 U.S.C. §§ 1501-1508 and 7324-7328) which limit the political activities of employees whose principal employment activities are funded in whole or in part with Federal funds.
9. Will comply, as applicable, with the provisions of the Davis-Bacon Act (40 U.S.C. §§ 276a to 276a-7), the Copeland Act (40 U.S.C. § 276c and 18 U.S.C. §§ 874), and the Contract Work Hours and Safety Standards Act (40 U.S.C. §§ 327-333), regarding labor standards for federally assisted construction subagreements.

Standard Form 424B (4-88)
Prescribed by OMB Circular A-102

Authorized for Local Reproduction

Figure 4-4. Sample assurances form.

10. Will comply, if applicable, with flood insurance purchase requirements of Section 102(a) of the Flood Disaster Protection Act of 1973 (P.L. 93-234) which requires recipients in a special flood hazard area to participate in the program andto purchase flood insurance if the total cost of insurable construction and acquisition is $10,000 or more.

11. Will comply with environmental standards which may be prescribed pursuant to the following: (a) institution of environmental quality control measures under the National Environmental Policy Act of 1969 (P.L. 91-190) and Executive Order (EO) 11514; (b) notification of violating facilities pursuant to EO 11738; (c) protection of wetlands pursuant to EO 11990; (d) evaluation of flood hazards in floodplains in accordance with EO 11988; (e) assurance of project consistency with the approved State management program developed under the Coastal Zone Management Act of 1972 (16 U.S.C. §§ 1451 et seq.); (f) conformity of Federal actions to State (Clear Air) Implementation Plans under Section 176(c) of the Clear Air Act of 1955, as amended (42 U.S.C. § 7401 et seq.); (g) protection of underground sources of drinking water under the Safe Drinking Water Act of 1974, as amended, (P.L. 93-523); and (h) protection of endangered species under the Endangered Species Act of 1973, as amended, (P.L. 93-205).

12. Will comply with the Wild and Scenic Rivers Act of 1968 (16 U.S.C. §§ 1271 et seq.) related to protecting components or potential components of the national wild and scenic rivers system.

13. Will assist the awarding agency in assuring compliance with Section 106 of the National Historic Preservation Act of 1966, as amended (16 U.S.C. 470), EO 11593 (identification and protection of historic properties), and the Archaeological and Historic Preservation Act of 1974 (16 U.S.C. 469a-1 et seq.).

14. Will comply with P.L. 93-348 regarding the protection of human subjects involved in research, development, and related activities supported by this award of assistance.

15. Will comply with the Laboratory Animal Welfare Act of 1966 (P.L. 89-544, as amended, 7 U.S.C. 2131 et seq.) pertaining to the care, handling, and treatment of warm blooded animals held for research, teaching, or other activities supported by this award of assistance.

16. Will comply with the Lead-Based Paint Poisoning Prevention Act (42 U.S.C. §§ 4801 et seq.) which prohibits the use of lead based paint in construction or rehabilitation of residence structures.

17. Will cause to be performed the required financial and compliance audits in accordance with the Single Audit Act of 1984.

18. Will comply with all applicable requirements of all other Federal laws, executive orders, regulations and policies governing this program.

SIGNATURE OF AUTHORIZED CERTIFYING OFFICIAL	TITLE
APPLICANT ORGANIZATION	DATE SUBMITTED

Figure 4-4 (*Continued*)

Certification Regarding Debarment, Suspension, and Other Responsibility Matters Primary Covered Transactions

This certification is required by the regulations implementing Executive Order 12549, Debarment and Suspension, 34 CFR Part 85, Section 85.510, Participants' responsibilities. The regulations were published as Part VII of the May 26, 1988 Federal Register (pages 19160-19211). Copies of the regulations may be obtained by contacting the U.S. Department of Education, Grants and Contracts Service, 400 Maryland Avenue, S.W. (Room 3633 GSA Regional Office Building No. 3), Washington, D.C. 20202-4725, telephone (202) 732-2505.

(BEFORE COMPLETING CERTIFICATION, READ INSTRUCTIONS ON REVERSE)

(1) The prospective primary participant certifies to the best of its knowledge and belief, that it and its principals:

(a) Are not presently debarred, suspended, proposed for debarment, declared ineligible, or voluntarily excluded from covered transactions by any Federal department or agency;

(b) Have not within a three-year period preceding this proposal been convicted of or had a civil judgment rendered against them for commission of fraud or a criminal offense in connection with obtaining, attempting to obtain, or performing a public (Federal, State or local) transaction or contract under a public transaction; violation of Federal or State antitrust statutes or commission of embezzlement, theft, forgery, bribery, falsification or destruction of records, making false statements, or receiving stolen property;

(c) Are not presently indicted for or otherwise criminally or civilly charged by a governmental entity (Federal, State or local) with commission of any of the offenses enumerated in paragraph (1)(b) of this certification; and

(d) Have not within a three-year period preceding this application/proposal had one or more public transactions (Federal, State or local) terminated for cause or default.

(2) Where the prospective primary participant is unable to certify to any of the statements in this certification, such prospective participant shall attach an explanation to this proposal.

____

Organization Name PR/Award Number or Project Name

____

Name and Title of Authorized Representative

____

Signature Date

ED Form GCS-008, (REV.12/88)

Figure 4-5. Sample certification form.

Federal Register / Vol. 54, No. 169 / Friday, September 1, 1989 / Notices 36733

Certification Regarding Drug-Free Workplace Requirements Grantees Other Than Individuals

This certification is required by the regulations implementing the Drug-Free Workplace Act of 1988, 34 CFR Part 85, Subpart F. The regulations, published in the January 31, 1989 Federal Register, require certification by grantees, prior to award, that they will maintain a drug-free workplace. The certification set out below is a material representation of fact upon which reliance will be placed when the agency determines to award the grant. False certification or violation of the certification shall be grounds for suspension of payments, suspension or termination of grants, or governmentwide suspension or debarment (see 34 CFR Part 85, Sections 85.615 and 85.620).

The grantee certifies that it will provide a drug-free workplace by:

(a) Publishing a statement notifying employees that the unlawful manufacture, distribution, dispensing, possession or use of a controlled substance is prohibited in the grantee's workplace and specifying the actions that will be taken against employees for violation of such prohibition;

(b) Establishing a drug-free awareness program to inform employees about--

(1) The dangers of drug abuse in the workplace;
(2) The grantee's policy of maintaining a drug-free workplace;
(3) Any available drug counseling, rehabilitation, and employee assistance programs; and
(4) The penalties that may be imposed upon employees for drug abuse violations occurring in the workplace;

(c) Making it a requirement that each employee to be engaged in the performance of the grant be given a copy of the statement required by paragraph (a);

(d) Notifying the employee in the statement required by paragraph (a) that, as a condition of employment under the grant, the employee will--

(1) Abide by the terms of the statement; and
(2) Notify the employer of any criminal drug statute conviction for a violation occurring in the workplace no later than five days after such conviction;

(e) Notifying the agency within ten days after receiving notice under subparagraph (d)(2) from an employee or otherwise receiving actual notice of such conviction;

(f) Taking one of the following actions, within 30 days of receiving notice under subparagraph (d)(2), with respect to any employee who is so convicted--

(1) Taking appropriate personnel action against such an employee, up to and including termination; or
(2) Requiring such employee to participate satisfactorily in a drug abuse assistance or rehabilitation program approved for such purposes by a Federal, State, or local health, law enforcement, or other appropriate agency;

(g) Making a good faith effort to continue to maintain a drug-free workplace through implementation of paragraphs (a), (b), (c), (d), (e) and (f).

Organization Name PR/Award Number or Project Name

Name and Title of Authorized Representative

Signature Date

ED 80-0004
[FR Doc. 89-20584 Filed 8-31-89; 8:45 am]
BILLING CODE 4000-01-C

Figure 4-6. Sample drug-free workplace certification.

Department of Health and Human Services
Public Health Service

Statement of Non-Delinquency On Federal Debt

Applicant's Name	Taxpayer I.D. Number (Social Security No. if the applicant is an individual)	PHS Grant No.

Instructions:

The applicant or, if the applicant is not an individual, the applicant's authorized representative, must complete and forward this sheet with the application and required documents. Please check the appropriate box below. If the "Yes" box is checked, please provide an explanation in the space provided. The question applies only to the person or institution requesting financial assistance, and does not apply to the person who signs an application form as the authorized representative of an institution or on behalf of another person who actually receives the funds.

Examples of Federal Debt include delinquent taxes, audit disallowances, guaranteed or direct student loans, FHA loans, business loans, and other miscellaneous administrative debts. For purposes of this certification, the following definitions of "delinquency" apply:

- For ***direct loans and fellowships*** *(whether awarded directly to the applicant by the Federal Government or by an instition using Federal funds)*, a debt more than 31 days past due on a scheduled financial payment. (This definition *excludes* "service" payback under a National Research Service Award.)
- For ***guaranteed and insured loans***, recipients of a loan guaranteed by the Federal Government that the Federal Government has repurchased from a lender because the borrower breached the loan agreement and is in default.
- For ***grants***, organizations in receipt of a "Notice of Grants Cost Disallowance" which have not repaid the disallowed amount or which have not resolved the disallowance. (This definition *excludes* disallowances in an "appeal" status.)

Is the applicant delinquent on the repayment of any Federal debt(s)?

☐ **NO** ☐ **YES** → *If your response was "Yes," please provide an explanation in the space provided below.*

I verify that the information provided above is true and complete to the best of my knowledge and belief.	Signature of Applicant or Applicant's Representative	Date

PHS-T-600 (7/88)

Figure 4-7. Sample form on debt to government.

DISCLOSURE OF LOBBYING ACTIVITIES

Approved by OMB 0348-0046

Complete this form to disclose lobbying activities pursuant to 31 U.S.C. 1352
(See reverse for public burden disclosure.)

1. Type of Federal Action:
☐ a. contract
b. grant
c. cooperative agreement
d. loan
e. loan guarantee
f. loan insurance

2. Status of Federal Action:
☐ a. bid/offer/application
b. initial award
c. post-award

3. Report Type:
☐ a. initial filing
b. material change
For Material Change Only:
year ______ quarter ____
date of last report ______

4. Name and Address of Reporting Entity:
☐ Prime ☐ Subawardee
Tier ____, *if known*:

Congressional District, *if known*:

5. If Reporting Entity in No. 4 is Subawardee, Enter Name and Address of Prime:

Congressional District, *if known*:

6. Federal Department/Agency:

7. Federal Program Name/Description:

CFDA Number, *if applicable*: ________

8. Federal Action Number, *if known*:

9. Award Amount, *if known*:
$

10. a. Name and Address of Lobbying Entity *(if individual, last name, first name, MI)*:

b. Individuals Performing Services *(including address if different from No. 10a)* *(last name, first name, MI)*:

(attach Continuation Sheet(s) SF-LLL-A, if necessary)

11. Amount of Payment *(check all that apply)*:
$ ____________ ☐ actual ☐ planned

12. Form of Payment *(check all that apply)*:
☐ a. cash
☐ b. in-kind; specify: nature ____________
value ____________

13. Type of Payment *(check all that apply)*:
☐ a. retainer
☐ b. one-time fee
☐ c. commission
☐ d. contingent fee
☐ e. deferred
☐ f. other; specify: ____________

14. Brief Description of Services Performed or to be Performed and Date(s) of Service, including officer(s), employee(s), or Member(s) contacted, for Payment Indicated in Item 11:

(attach Continuation Sheet(s) SF-LLL-A, if necessary)

15. Continuation Sheet(s) SF-LLL-A attached: ☐ Yes ☐ No

16. Information requested through this form is authorized by title 31 U.S.C. section 1352. This disclosure of lobbying activities is a material representation of fact upon which reliance was placed by the tier above when this transaction was made or entered into. This disclosure is required pursuant to 31 U.S.C. 1352. This information will be reported to the Congress semi-annually and will be available for public inspection. Any person who fails to file the required disclosure shall be subject to a civil penalty of not less than $10,000 and not more than $100,000 for each such failure.

Signature: ____________
Print Name: ____________
Title: ____________
Telephone No.: ________ **Date:** ________

Federal Use Only:

Authorized for Local Reproduction
Standard Form - LLL

Figure 4-8. Sample form on lobbying.

Two caveats should be taken into account in following this approach, however. First, be aware that readers are not obligated to read *anything* added in this way. Nothing should be included in the appendix which is essential to your case, for it may be totally overlooked. Second, consider the possibility that adding too much material can actually work against you. Readers may become annoyed by what they consider information overkill or a blatant attempt to get around length requirements. To avoid this problem, be sure to read application instructions very carefully, and take into account statements or hints that appendixes are not allowed or simply not encouraged.

3. *To reinforce key points.* As discussed more fully in the next chapter, it sometimes helps to repeat key points in different sections of the proposal to make sure that readers do not miss them. The appendix can also be used for this purpose. For example, extra charts or graphs can be added to amplify material in the main body of the proposal. Or the appendix may include an excerpt of an article or report which has been cited in the narrative.

4. *To meet proposal requirements.* Occasionally, an appendix will be required rather than optional. If so, this will be stated in the instructions. When this happens, be sure to follow the instructions just as you would for any other proposal component, and include all materials noted.

5. *To "pad" the proposal.* This is the least valid reason for adding material. Proposal writers sometimes add an extensive appendix to lengthen a proposal which seems too short. Appearances may be improved in such instances, but few readers will be fooled by this technique. Padding of this type is often futile.

Where it *may* help, on the other hand, is with a proposal that is already comprehensive. Sometimes, well-developed proposals may be enhanced by adding even more material, within reasonable limits. But even here information overkill is not generally a good idea.

Other Proposal Elements

Other proposal elements may be required in some proposals or added in others at the author's discretion. For example, a research proposal may include a comprehensive review of the published literature in the area where additional research is being proposed. Or a proposal for a training project may include a listing of courses or seminars to be offered, with a complete description of the content of each course.

While proposal formats may vary, it is hard to go wrong if you follow the following steps:

1. *Read application instructions carefully, including all the "fine print."*

2. *Make a rough outline of the contents before beginning the development of the application*

3. *Be willing to exceed the minimum.* It is important not only to address each point where information is requested but to respond as fully as possible. Remember, the written proposal will have to stand on its own during the review process. It can be only as complete as you make it.

4. *Think competitively.* In most cases, more applicants will be turned down than will be funded. In some cases, only a small proportion—or only a single proposal—will receive funding. Try to make yours as complete and thorough as possible to strengthen its chances against those of other applicants.

A Sample Grant Proposal

A sample grant proposal is given in Fig. 4-9. Please note that for the sake of brevity this proposal does not include some of the forms and other materials described in this chapter. But it does include the major proposal sections found in many proposals.

As previously mentioned, proposal lengths vary widely. The application shown in Fig. 4-9 is neither particularly long nor especially short. It is offered not as a model to be copied or emulated but simply as a representative example of an ordinary proposal; in other words, to provide you with an idea of what might be covered in a typical grant proposal.

Proposals for research projects tend to include more technical information such as scientific literature reviews, technical drawings or illustrations, chemical or mathematical formulas, and so forth. Proposals for contracts can be divided into technical and business proposals, and they contain more forms and fill-in-the-blank-type information than do the unified, persuasive proposals required for most grants (see the sample contract RFP in App. D for comparison). At any rate, it is uncommon for any two proposals to follow identical formats. The proposal developer should be both aware of such differences and prepared to adapt techniques from one type of proposal to another.

Part I - Federal Assistance Face Sheet

OMB Approval No. 0348-0043

APPLICATION FOR FEDERAL ASSISTANCE

1. TYPE OF SUBMISSION: *Application* ☐ Construction ☒ Non-Construction; *Preapplication* ☐ Construction ☒ Non-Construction	2. DATE SUBMITTED 9-9-89	Applicant Identifier
	3. DATE RECEIVED BY STATE	State Application Identifier
	4. DATE RECEIVED BY FEDERAL AGENCY	Federal Identifier

5. APPLICANT INFORMATION

Legal Name: CDR, Inc.	Organizational Unit: Same
Address (*give city, county, state, and zip code*): 224 Oak Lane, Dublin, NC 25402	Name and telephone number of the person to be contacted on matters involving this application (*give area code*): Mark C. Allen (704) 555-2349

6. EMPLOYER IDENTIFICATION NUMBER (EIN): 243 – 5 6 6 2 0 0 H

7. TYPE OF APPLICANT: (*enter appropriate letter in box*) M

A. State; B. County; C. Municipal; D. Township; E. Interstate; F. Intermunicipal; G. Special District; H. Independent School Dist.; I. State Controlled Institution of Higher Learning; J. Private University; K. Indian Tribe; L. Individual; M. Profit Organization; N. Other (Specify): ______

8. TYPE OF APPLICATION: ☐ New ☐ Continuation ☐ Revision

If Revision, enter appropriate letter(s) in box(es): ☐ ☐

A. Increase Award B. Decrease Award C. Increase Duration D. Decrease Duration Other (*specify*): ______

9. NAME OF FEDERAL AGENCY: U.S. DEPARTMENT OF EDUCATION

10. CATALOG OF FEDERAL DOMESTIC ASSISTANCE NUMBER: 8 4 . 1 9 3

TITLE: PROJECT "Help"

11. DESCRIPTIVE TITLE OF APPLICANT'S PROJECT: Comprehensive prógram for the retraining of dislocated workers

12. AREAS AFFECTED BY PROJECT (*cities, counties, states, etc.*): Four counties in Western NC

13. PROPOSED PROJECT: Start Date	Ending Date	14. CONGRESSIONAL DISTRICTS OF: a. Applicant	b. Project
7-90	6-91	Fifth	Fifth

15. ESTIMATED FUNDING:

a. Federal	$ 96, 692 .00
b. Applicant	$ .00
c. State	$ .00
d. Local	$ .00
e. Other	$ .00
f. Program Income	$ .00
g. TOTAL	$ 96, 692 .00

16. IS APPLICATION SUBJECT TO REVIEW BY STATE EXECUTIVE ORDER 12372 PROCESS?

a. YES. THIS PREAPPLICATION/APPLICATION WAS MADE AVAILABLE TO THE STATE EXECUTIVE ORDER 12372 PROCESS FOR REVIEW ON: DATE ______

b. NO. ☐ PROGRAM IS NOT COVERED BY E.O. 12372 ☐ OR PROGRAM HAS NOT BEEN SELECTED BY STATE FOR REVIEW

17. IS THE APPLICANT DELINQUENT ON ANY FEDERAL DEBT? ☐ Yes If "Yes," attach an explanation. ☐ No

18. TO THE BEST OF MY KNOWLEDGE AND BELIEF, ALL DATA IN THIS APPLICATION/PREAPPLICATION ARE TRUE AND CORRECT, THE DOCUMENT HAS BEEN DULY AUTHORIZED BY THE GOVERNING BODY OF THE APPLICANT AND THE APPLICANT WILL COMPLY WITH THE ATTACHED ASSURANCES IF THE ASSISTANCE IS AWARDED

a. Typed Name of Authorized Representative: Mark C. Allen	b. Title: President	c. Telephone number: 555-2349
d. Signature of Authorized Representative: Mark C. Allen		e. Date Signed

Previous Editions Not Usable

Standard Form 424 (REV 4-88) Prescribed by OMB Circular A-102

Authorized for Local Reproduction

Figure 4-9. Sample grant proposal.

ABSTRACT

Project "HELP" is an outgrowth of a cooperative plan among industrial, educational, and governmental leaders in a four-county area of western North Carolina. The project was designed by the applicant, CDR, Inc., to encourage a resuscitation of the heartbeat of the work force in the area while, at the same time, providing a tested model which can be replicated by other dislocated worker programs in the country.

Project Objectives

1. To operate a regional demonstration center which provides both training and resource services for dislocated workers and employers.
2. To provide resource services and occupational skills training, including literacy and basic skills instruction, were needed, for a minimum of 150 dislocated workers in order to foster the development of their marketable skills.
3. To disseminate oral and written information to project participants and employers about (a) current job market conditions in the area, (b) educational and vocational training opportunities available at local community colleges, (c) techniques for effective job search and job retention.
4. To provide, through a monthly support group/workshop session, professional development activities for project participants.
5. To provide individual counseling or counseling referrals for dislocated workers who need assistance in dealing with personal, educational and occupational concerns.
6. To network the center with services provided by public and private agencies within the community.
7. To disseminate information about the model program to other agencies who are designing their own dislocated worker programs.

Project Participants

Project "Help" will serve (a) a minimum of 100 dislocated workers through its resource services component, and (b) a minimum of 50 dislocated workers through its occupational skills training component.

Figure 4-9 (*Continued*)

Expected Outcomes

As a result of the project, a minimum of 75 percent of the project participants will return to the workforce immediately following training. In addition, the center will become the facilitator of a systematic, coordinated, and comprehensive resource network for area services available for dislocated workers. It will become a demonstration model for serving, in a caring and creative environment, the occupational and personal needs of dislocated workers.

Figure 4-9 *(Continued)*

A COMPREHENSIVE PROGRAM FOR THE RETRAINING OF DISLOCATED WORKERS

INTRODUCTION

The announcement of Smith Mills' plans to close in spring 1988 was a staggering blow to its 600 workers and to Putnam County as well; then that first impact was followed by alternating optimism and discouragement among Smith employees as they heard rumors about possible buyouts and then realized that the rumors were unfounded. These workers were torn about whether to search for one of the few available jobs in the textile industry or whether to change vocations, quite a challenge for the middle-aged workers who had been employed at Smith for most of their working lives. Their decisions were made more difficult with the realization that their early departure from the plant would mean a loss of the few retirement benefits that they would receive from the company if they stayed until the plant closed its doors.

Similar dramas have been replayed many times during recent years in western North Carolina. After Smith closed its manufacturing plant, Johnson Textile followed later in the same year, leaving 350 more workers unemployed. Then came an announcement of the impending close of another textile facility in the region. The closing of this plant, Ford Jeans, would add 300 more names to the list of dislocated workers in the region. These layoffs and others contributed to a local unemployment rate which far exceeded that of the rest of the state and the nation.

Fortunately, the picture has not been one of total bleakness within the area, for there has been an increase in the number of available jobs in the area. But in order for dislocated workers to be able to fit into these jobs, they often need as-

Figure 4-9 (*Continued*)

sistance; and this assistance must come in the form of a comprehensive, systematic effort among education, business, and government.

Project "Help" is the result of a cooperative effort to resuscitate the heartbeat of the work force of the western North Carolina region while, at the same time, providing a tested model which can be replicated by other dislocated worker programs in the United States.

APPLICANT BACKGROUND

CRD (Career Resource Development), Inc., is a firm specializing in career conseling, testing research, skill development, training, and related services. Founded in 1984, the company is staffed by two full-time professionals, two clerical personnel and three part-time professionals. CRD has established an excellent working relationship with schools, community colleges, literacy organizations and business concerns throughout western North Carolina.

CRD is experienced in receiving and managing federal funds. The firm has received an SBIR award through the U.S. Department of Education, four contracts under the Job Training Partnership Act, and several other contracts and sub-contracts.

NEED FOR PROJECT

The economy of the area is based primarily on the manufacture of durable and nondurable goods (textiles, furniture, automotive parts, for example). Considering the entire country's move from a manufacturing to a service economy, it is not too surprising that the college's service region is facing a major challenge with its increasing numbers of dislocated workers.

During the time period from the first quarter of 1985 to the fourth quarter of 1988, each area in the four-county region suffered a significant loss of jobs within at least one of its major companies. Putnam County suffered the greatest loss.

Figure 4-9 *(Continued)*

Of its 20 major employers, four--Smith Mills, Johnson Textile, Ford Jeans and ATL--were forced to lay off approximately 2,300 workers, leaving the county with an unemployment rate of 11 percent. Three Mercer County companies also experienced significant losses in their number of employees, and Cloyd County saw the loss of 178 positions within a textile company, Harbor Garment. In addition, Webster County saw the loss of 195 positions from two different firms. These 3,000+ dislocated workers represent 35 percent of these comapnies' first quarter 1985 total work force.

Since January 1989, the population of dislocated workers in the region has continued to increase as a result of 409 permanent layoffs. June 1989 unemployment rates which were distributed by the state employment commission showed the effect of this continuing problem. Webster County had a 9.8 percent unemployment rate; Putnam County, 7.0; Mercer County, 6.1; and Cloyd County, 5.2. These figures contrasted greatly with the state figure of 3.6 percent for the same time period.

This picture is especially poignant in light of two factors. First, the region's adults are poorly educated compared to other Americans. According to 1980 census figures, only 48 percent of area residents 25 years of age and older had completed high school, compared to 65 percent for the state and 67 percent for the U.S. Second, rural locations and lack of industrial diversity make it hard for workers to find new job opportunities, but rural workers bring many strong qualities to the job when they do. They make good employees because they have excellent work habits. Citizens of the region have always been noted for their strong work ethic, a quality that is often noted by manufacturers who decide to locate in the area.

Figure 4-9 *(Continued)*

Having maintained a close relationship with businesses, industries, and citizens in its service region, CDR naturally shares the concerns about dislocated workers; however, it also recognizes some inherent opportunities. Fortunately for the area citizens, there are jobs available if the prospective employees have the appropriate skills and/or training. A coordinated, comprehensive program of employment preparation and skills training such as the one proposed could significantly increase the employability of dislocated workers in the region.

PLAN OF OPERATION

Philosophy

The design for the proposed project is based on nine precepts:

A center for the retraining of dislocated workers should

- Be a cooperative effort among education, business, and government.
- Be both a training and resource center.
- Help prevent the dislocation of workers, while recognizing at the same time that some industries are bound to decline and should be allowed to do so.
- Encourage as much lead time as possible in the dislocation of workers to allow for their retraining prior to unemployment.
- Attempt to enhance existing skills rather than starting over.
- Promote an understanding that skillls do not last a lifetime and that lifelong learning is necessary.
- Assure equal access to traditionally underrepresented groups.
- Attempt to offset economic or family crisis situations which hinder a person's employability.
- Operate with compassion and creativity.

Goals and Objectives

The goals and objectives of the Comprehensive Program for the Retraining of Dislocated Workers (PROJECT HELP) include the following:

Figure 4-9 *(Continued)*

1. **To operate a regional demonstration center which provides both training and resource services for dislocated workers and employers in the region.** This center will facilitate--through education, counseling, information dissemination, and coordination of education, government, and community services--the reentry of dislocated workers into the local workforce.

2. **To provide resource services and occupational training, including basic skills instruction where needed, for 150 clients in order to foster the development of their marketable skills.** Through funding by the grant or other sources, these participants will be awarded financial assistance for tuition and fees, for textbooks and other required class materials, and for their general subsistance in order to eliminate barriers to their participation in the program

3. **To disseminate oral and written information to project participants and employers about (a) current job market conditions in the region (b) educational and vocational training opportunities available at the community college, (c) techniques for effective job search and job retention.**

4. **To provide, through a monthly support group/workshop session, professional development activities for project participants.** Workshop topics will include resume preparation, interviewing skills, effective academic strategies, job market trends, and equity issues.

5. **To provide individual counseling or counseling referrals for dislocated workers who need assistance in dealing with personal and educational-related problems, as well as with job search support.**

6. **To network the center with services provided by agencies within the community.**

7. **To disseminate information about the model program to other agencies who are designing their own dislocated worker programs.** There will be ongoing publicity for the center, including a brochure, newsletter, informational flyers, and new releases.

Project Management

The Center will be under the direct management of a full-time project director and a half-time secretary. The project director will report to the Director of Special Projects (see organizational chart in Appendix) and will implement all aspects of the project, including adherence to state and federal government policies and procedures for fiscal management, monitoring, and reporting.

Figure 4-9 (*Continued*)

Assisting with the management of the center will be an advisory committee consisting of college resource personnel from two local community colleges (Green River Community College and Baker Community College) as well as four county administrators from the region, a city manager, three representatives from businesses/industries, and a state employment commission representative.

Resource Services

The proposed program will serve as both a resource center and training center. Services of the resource center will be available to all dislocated workers and employers in the region. Because of budgetary constraints, services of the training center will be available to 50 clients in this model program. As a resource center, the office will provide information about, and referral to, all programs and services that exist in the area--employment services programs, Job Training Partnership Act services, Trade Readjustment Act training, social services, veterans' services, and unemployment compensation. Additionally, information on all local vocational education programs and available rehabilitation programs will be provided through the resource center services. Clients' eligibility and/or certification for college and community services will typically be determined during initial contact with the center. If further information not available in the center is needed by a client, the project director will help make contacts with the appropriate individuals or agencies.

The resource center will maintain a library of printed information about the center itself, about other agencies in the community which can provide services to dislocated workers, about relevant media presentations or workshops in the area, about the job market, and about successful job search and job retention.

The center will also serve as a resource agency for businesses and industries which are facing economic pressures. The project director will refer, where

Figure 4-9 (*Continued*)

appropriate, business/industry representatives to local community colleges, literacy organization or other appropriate agencies.

Counseling and Training Services

Counseling and training activities for clients will include the following:

1) Pre-employment counseling will be provided to members of the target group needing such assistance;
2) During the counseling process, information will be provided on educational and career options available to each client;
3) All persons desiring assistance will be given help in job development including instruction in resume development, interviewing skills, and related areas.
4) Where background and interest are considered appropriate by both client and the project staff, individuals will be placed in educational/training programs offered by local institutions. This will include programs in Basic Education, high school completion, improvement of academic skills, and/or academic programs at the certificate or degree level in a variety of technical and non-traditional areas. CRD will serve as a broker for such services, assessing client needs and then assisting them in appropriate placement.

In support of these activities, employability development and supportive services activities will be ongoing. Continuous components which will commence immediately following the assessment process and end with job placement. The project director will meet regularly with each individual in the project to track the progress of that individual and to identify the need for referral to other agencies for assistance.

Assessment/referral. Prospective clients will be identified by business and industries who are cutting back their work force, by the state employment

Figure 4-9 (*Continued*)

Commission, and through individual response to advertisements about the program. During the pre-assessment interview, they will be given information about the center and, if appropriate, will be referred to other community agencies as described previously. The project director will interview prospective project participants to identify any barriers which would hinder their attainment of training objectives and to determine their need for supportive services which could reduce and/or eliminate these barriers. Referral to appropriate supportive services will then be made. Assessment tools (including the General Aptitude Test Battery and the Test of Adult Basic Education) will be used to determine clients' reading and math levels, as well as their vocational aptitudes and interests. Clients who enter below second-grade proficiency in reading will be tested with a standard literacy instrument, such as the READ test (Reading Evaluation Adult Diagnosis, by Literacy Volunteers of America).

Employability development. Through its existing resources, CDR is able to offer clients a strong career planning component. Among the resource materials available in the center is DISCOVER for Adult Learners, an information delivery system for self, career, college, and job exploration. Other resource materials include the state Job Bank, which is a weekly listing of job openings in the state and the nation, career pamphlets, magazines, books, and corporate literature. CDR also sponsors an annual career day program in cooperation with local educational institutions for the purpose of providing information about businesses and industries, as well as scheduling interviews.

Project staff will develop an individualized employability development plan will be prepared for each project participant. This plan will be based on assessment data, including goals established by the individual, barriers to employment, and the need for supportive services. Project staff will review and update these

Figure 4-9 *(Continued)*

individualized plans each month as they chart individual progress toward goals. As needs dictate, project staff will refer individuals to other agencies for assistance.

During the time of the project, participants will also receive employability training through a monthly support group/workshop session. Discussion topics will include job search and interview skills; job retention skills, including developing an awareness of employer expectations and methods for managing stress on the job; and personal and family improvement skills. As needs dictate, additional topics for workshops will be included in the employability development training.

Remedial/basic skills training. Often, displaced workers have no high school diploma, and many have very low basic skills levels as well. Since some of the industries replacing the manufacturing industries will likely be information industries, it may be necessary for some clients to receive some basic skills training prior to entering occupational training. Basic skills training for the project participants will be determined according to their ability and prior educational background, as revealed during the assessment process. This training will be provided through literacy volunteer groups, adult basic education, GED training, and through remedial classes at the community college. In addition, the project participants will have access, at CDR, to a new computer-based remedial self-paced education program. Software purchased for this program will cover a variety of skills levels, from basic reading, writing, and math instruction to others geared toward specific occupations.

Occupational skills training. The occupational skills training will be based upon clients' interests, aptitudes, and the availability of local programs. Project participants will be directed toward those programs which will enhance the skills

Figure 4-9 *(Continued)*

that they already possess, as well as toward those which would offer employment opportunities in the region. Occupational curricula which have already been identified as those which will offer employment in the region over the next decade include the following certificate programs (all are nine-month programs except the licensed practical nursing program, which covers a twelve-month period): accounting, accounting clerk/typist, business and industrial supervision, clerical studies, clerk/stenographer, computer operations, drafting and design, fashion merchandising, forensic science, industrial maintenance, law enforcement, licensed practical nursing, records management, and word processing. These certificate programs have been designed by the local community colleges in conjunction with advisory boards consisting of personnel in the specific occupations who constantly review and validate the program requirements.

Placement. At the end of the occupational training, project participants will be referred to job openings which are congruent with their training. They will be assisted in finding these jobs by project staff and the state employment commission.

QUALITY OF TRAINING

All training within the proposed project will be conducted by qualified personnel. Literacy training will be conducted through literacy volunteer organizations; adult basic education and GED training will be conducted by certified professionals within the client's county or city; and remedial or basic skills training will be conducted by community college instructors at the college in a caring, small-class environment (15-25 students). Tutorial services will be available for those students who need extra help. The remedial/basic skills instructors at the colleges are accustomed to working with students who have special needs,

Figure 4-9 *(Continued)*

especially adults who have been out of the mainstream of education for some time.

Although a transfer curriculum may be an option for a few of the project participants, most will enter a curriculum which will enable them to return to the work force as soon as possible. Available choices atthe two participating community colleges will be thirty-eight occupational/technical certificate, diploma, and degree curricula, including the following:

Associate Degree	Certificate	Diploma
Accounting	Accounting	Automotive Technology
Architectural Technology	Accounting Clerk/Typist	Automotive Analysis & Repair
Business Management	Business and Industrial	Sign Communication
Child Care	Child Care	Machine Operations
Community & Social Services	Clerical Studies	
Computer Information Systems Technology	Clerk Stenographer	
Drafting & Design	Community & Social Services	
Electrical Technology	Computer Operations	
Electronics Technology	Drafting & Design	
Forensic Science	Fashion Merchandising	
Industrial Engineering Technician	Forensic Science	
Instrumentation Technology	Industrial maintenance	
Machine Technology	Law Enforcement	
Marketing	Practical Nursing	
Nursing	Records Management	
Office Systems Technology	Welding	
Police Science	Word Processing	
Word Processing		

Project participants may also be able to take advantage of special training programs that the two colleges frequently offer as specific job opportunities become available. These programs, which are usually of a short-term nature, are tailored to fit the exact needs of a company and are terminated when employment needs and objectives have been met. Examples of these short-term programs have included the following: Accounts Receivable/Accounts Payable; Automotive Chassis Mechanics; Automotive Engines; Automotive Power Trains; Banking and Financial Management programs, including Commercial Lending,

Figure 4-9 *(Continued)*

Consumer Credit, and Mortgage Lending; Computer Applications; Cost Accounting Clerk; Data Entry; Fire Science; Payroll Clerk; Production and Inventory Management; Quality Control; Refrigeration and Air Conditioning; Salesmanship; and Supervisory Development.

Dislocated workers who successfully complete any of the occupational/technical programs offered by the local colleges will likely find employment, for all programs are planned in light of the labor market and in close coordination with the business community through a business/industry needs assessment conducted by the college at regular intervals. (See "Employment Opportunities" section.) As mentioned earlier, the content of each occupational/technical curriculum is regularly validated by an advisory committee who reviews the technical classes in light of technical advances and employment trends.

National statistics for certain jobs which do not require a bachelor's degree and which will experience a significant growth rate to the year 2000 support the potential of the programs listed above: licensed practical nurses, nursing aides, general office clerks, receptionists, guards, first-line supervisors and managers, marketing personnel, computer operators, computer programmers, social workers, advertising managers, accountants, and electrical and electronics technicians. (Occupational Projections and Data, Bulletin 2301, U.S. Department of Labor, April 1988).

As is indicated throughout the description of the project, counseling is a strong component of the project. One of the criteria for the selection of the project director will be a background in counseling. The assessment activities described earlier will help assure that clients will enter training in which they have both aptitude and interest. (See resume in Appendix) The project director will guide the project participants to the free services for career and life planning ser-

Figure 4-9 *(Continued)*

vices provided through this grant and elsewhere. Because dislocation from the workforce is inevitably accompanied by personal adjustments and traumas, personal counseling will also be available to clients, either through the project director, support group/workshop sessions, college counseling staff, or referral to community agencies. In addition to the individual counseling and support group meetings, an open forum for dislocated workers and their families will be held twice each year. Speakers will address the group about family members' roles in coping with their changing lifestyle while helping to maintain personal and family health, about available supportive services for dislocated workers, and about other relevant topics.

Both the training and the counseling services provided through the project can help ensure workers being prepared to reenter the workforce.

QUALITY OF KEY PERSONNEL

The project director will be hired according to the following qualifications:

Percentage of time to be devoted to project: 100%

Special qualifications/experience:

Master's degree in counseling, adult education, community college education, or related area
Experience in program management
Strong human relations skills
Experience in working with dislocated workers and community agencies preferred
Experience in academic, career, and financial aid counseling preferred

In addition to the project director, a secretary will be hired to assist with the project. This person will be hired according to these qualifications:

Percentage of time to be devoted to the project: 50%

Special qualifications/experience:

Figure 4-9 *(Continued)*

Typing skills 45-50 works per minute
Data entry skills
Excellent communication skills
Strong human relations skills

Job vacancy announcements will be advertised in all newspapers that serve the region Additionally, all job vacancy announcements are sent to approximately 100 organizations for minorities.

It is the policy of CDR, Inc., to promote equal opportunity in educational programs and activities, admission, and employment without regard to race, creed, sex, national origin, age, handicap, or any other non-merit factor.

BUDGET

The budget for the proposed project is outlined on the forms which follow.

EVALUATION PLAN

The project will be assessed through summative and process evaluation methods. The evaluation will be primarily the responsibility of the project director, but an ongoing evaluation will also occur by means of quarterly meetings with the advisory committee, who will review the information provided by the project director and plan alternate strategies where necessary.

The project director will maintain documentation of the number of persons who use services of the resource center, either directly or through referral, and the number who receive training. Using feedback from meetings with clients, from class attendance records, from grade reports, from the use of supportive services, and from job placements, the project director will track the progress of each client in the training program. Additionally, the director will prepare quarterly reports which assess the progress of the project according to criteria for the

Figure 4-9 *(Continued)*

OMB Approval No. 0348-0044

BUDGET INFORMATION — Non-Construction Programs

SECTION A – BUDGET SUMMARY

Grant Program Function or Activity (a)	Catalog of Federal Domestic Assistance Number (b)	Estimated Unobligated Funds: Federal (c)	Estimated Unobligated Funds: Non-Federal (d)	New or Revised Budget: Federal (e)	New or Revised Budget: Non-Federal (f)	New or Revised Budget: Total (g)
1. Demonst. Center/ Dislocated Workers	84.193	$	$	$ 96,692	$	$ 96,692
2.						
3.						
4.						
5. TOTALS		$	$	$	$	$

SECTION B – BUDGET CATEGORIES

6 Object Class Categories	Grant Program, Function or Activity (1)	(2)	(3)	(4)	Total (5)
a. Personnel	$ 48,270	$	$	$	$
b. Fringe Benefits	13,033				
c. Travel	770				
d. Equipment	0				
e. Supplies	500				
f. Contractual	0				
g. Construction	0				
h. Other	26,957				
i. Total Direct Charges (sum of 6a - 6h)	89,530				
j. Indirect Charges	7,162				
k. TOTALS (sum of 6i and 6j)	$ 96,692	$	$	$	$
7. Program Income	$	$	$	$	$

Authorized for Local Reproduction

Standard Form 424A (4-88)
Prescribed by OMB Circular A-102

Figure 4-9 *(Continued)*

ADDITIONAL BUDGET INFORMATION

BUDGET ITEM	FUNDS REQUESTED
Personnel	
Project Director - 100%, 12 mo.	$36,000
Secretary - 100%, 12 mo.	12,270
Subtotal	48,270
Fringe Benefits @ 27% (Includes 12.51% for retirement; 7.65% for FICA; 1.02% for life insurance; 5.82% for health insurance)	13,033
Travel - Project Director	
Travel to Washington, D. C. for project director's conference	770
Supplies	
Miscellaneous office supplies	500
Other	
Publicity	
Brochure - 2 color, trifold (5,000)	1,500
Quarterly newsletter - 4 pages ea. (3,000)	1,000
Newspaper advertisements	2,000
Informational flyers	200
Tuition for Client Attendance at Local Community Colleges	
$26.60/cr. x 12 cr. x 1 sem. x 6	1,915
$26.60/cr. x 12 cr. x 1 sem. x 12	3,830
Fees	
$12/sem. x 1 sem. x 18	
Textbooks/Supplies	
$150/sem. x 1 sem. x 6	900
$150/sem. x 1 sem. x 18	2,700

Figure 4-9 (*Continued*)

BUDGET ITEM	FUNDS REQUESTED
GED Test $20 x 5	100
Client Stipends $3.50/hr. x 12 hr./wk. x 16 wks. x 18	12,096
Subtotal	26,957
Total Direct Charges	89,530
Indirect Charges @ 8%	7,162
TOTAL	$96,692

Figure 4-9 (*Continued*)

achievement of objectives (listed below). Any barriers to the progress of the project as outlined in the proposal will be documented, as will an explanation of any deviations from the proposed plan. Any particularly successful or unsuccessful components of the project will be documented. Since one of the purposes of the project is to serve as a demonstration program, information from these quarterly reports will be incorporated into the design of the instructional manual, which will be prepared as a part of the project activities and distributed to other agencies who are designing their own dislocated worker programs.

Specific criteria for the evaluation of each of the objective established for the project follow.

OBJECTIVE 1: To operate a regional demonstration center which provides both training and resource services for dislocated workers and employers.

Criteria for the Achievement of Objective

By July 1, 1990, the project director and secretary will be hired.

By September 1, 1990, the center will be operational. A brochure will be available for distribution, and advertisements about the program will be distributed to area businesses and industries, as well as to the agencies that will be networked with the project. Literacy providers will have been contacted; occupational and special training programs will have been identified for the training of the dislocated workers. The project director and secretary will maintain documentation of all these activities.

OBJECTIVE 2: To provide resource services and occupational training, including basic skills instruction where needed, for 150 clients in order to foster the development of their marketable skills.

Criteria for the Achievement of Objective

By June 1992, a minimum of 100 clients will have been served through resource center services, and an additional 50 clients will have completed training. Documentation will be maintained for each type of service. Of those receiving training, a minimum of 75 percent will have been placed in unsubsidized employment. Clients who have received training will have been awarded financial assistance for full tuition and fees, as well as for textbooks and other required class materials. Those whose unemploy-

Figure 4-9 *(Continued)*

ment compensation has been discontinued will have received a stipend for each hour spent n training.

OBJECTIVE 3: To disseminate oral and written information to project participants and employers about (a) current job market conditions in the New River Valley, (b) educational and vocational training opportunities available at the community college, (c) techniques for effective job search, and (d) job retention.

Criteria for the Achievement of Objective

By September 1, 1991, the printed materials mentioned above will be available for distribution. Then at the beginning of each month, the materials will be updated as needed. The project director and secretary will maintain documentation of (a) printed materials distributed through the center and (b) requests for information.

OBJECTIVE 4: To provide, through a monthly support group/workshop session, professional development activities for project participants.

Criteria for the Achievement of Objective

By June 30, 1992, a monthly support group/workshop will have been sponsored through the center. The project director and secretary will maintain documentation of topics and of participation in support group/workshop activities.

OBJECTIVE 5: To provide individual counseling or counseling referrals for participants who need assistance in dealing with personal problems, education-related problems, and job search support.

Criteria for the Achievement of Objective

As a part of the project design, counseling by the project director and college resource personnel will be an integral part of the project activities; however, all clients will receive information about additional counseling services that are available. If this additional counseling support is needed, the project director and secretary will maintain documentation of all referrals.

OBJECTIVE 6: To network the center with other special programs provided through the college.

Criteria for the Achievement of Objective

Prior to their entering training, each client will be informed (through information provided in the brochure, and through the assessment activities) of

Figure 4-9 (*Continued*)

other special programs which can also provide services. Documentation will be maintained of clients' participation in any of these special programs.

OBJECTIVE 7: To disseminate information about the model program to other agencies who are designing their own dislocated worker programs.

Criteria for the Achievement of Objective

By September 1, 1991, an instructional manual will be prepared and ready for distribution to other agencies involved in planning dislocated worker programs. The booklet will contain a basic design for such a program and will report on successful strategies for implementation.

By January 1, 1991; March 1, 1991, September 1, 1991; January 1, 1992, and March 1, 1992, a quarterly newsletter will have been published for distribution to other agencies who request information about the dislocated worker program.

ADEQUACY OF RESOURCES

The center will be housed at the offices of CDR, Inc., in Dublin, North Carolina. In addition to the personnel and educational resources already described, CDR will provide an office for the project director and secretary, the necessary office furniture, as well as typewriter, personal computer, and printer. The applicant will also provide telephone service, postal service, and postage fees for the distribution of materials.

DISSEMINATION

The project director and advisory committee, in conjunction with existing CDR staff, will design and produce a brochure which will describe the purpose and the services of the project. The brochure will be available for distribution at the center itself, as well as in key locations such as the state employment commission, other employment services agencies, and the community college. In addition, the brochure will be distributed to employers in the region, to civic organizations, and to social services and mental health agencies.

Figure 4-9 (*Continued*)

Information about the program will also be disseminated through paid advertisements and public service announcements in local media, as well as through a quarterly four-page newsletter published by the project director. The newsletter will provide information relevant to concerns of dislocated workers as well as success stories and features.

As a part of the pre-assessment interview procedure, clients will be asked how they heard of the program. This information will be documented in order for the project director and advisory committee to evaluate whether there are any segments of the service region that are not being reached.

Near the end of the project of the program, the project director and advisory committee, in conjunction with resource personnel for the project, will design and produce a "how to" book or instructional manual, which describes methodology for establishing a similar program for dislocated workers. Information in the book will be based on the successes and failures of the model program. The book will be advertised in the newsletter published by the center director and will be available upon request.

Figure 4-9 *(Continued)*

5 Submitting Proposals

Once an initial draft of your proposal has been completed, you can congratulate yourself on a significant achievement. But don't break out the champagne glasses yet—work still remains to be done. You will need to review the proposal, make any improvements that time allows, and then take the necessary steps to submit the application. Only then can the proposal development process be considered truly complete.

Revising and Enhancing Proposals

Knowing what to include in a grant or contract proposal is only part of the formula for success. *How* you present the information may be the most important factor of all. In most cases, your proposal will be submitted in competition with others. This can become a numbers game in which, quite often, the majority of applications are not successful.

To give your proposal the best possible chance of being selected for funding, take time to review your work and make every possible improvement. The most effective approach in developing a high-quality proposal is to write a rough draft first and then revise and improve the document in subsequent versions. While this is true for virtually any written effort, grant and contract proposals have their own special features which should be emphasized in the revision process.

An important point to remember is that proposals may not be read as thoroughly as one might assume. Even though you may put in a great deal of work preparing the most comprehensive application possible, readers may not give it the attention it merits; they may skim rather than carefully read each word.

This may not seem fair, but it becomes more understandable when you realize just how proposals are reviewed. In some cases, this review is conducted by a team of readers who have been retained by the government for the specific purpose of reviewing proposals for a particular competition. They may be college professors, consultants, or other "experts" in the field. Working in Washington motel rooms or conference rooms, they may be handed a huge stack of proposals and asked to rate each one within a period of just a few days. For example, say a three-person team is asked to evaluate 180 proposals which have been received for a particular program. Even if the team divides the work load, that means each individual must read and rate 60 proposals within a short time. In addition, reviewers may need to read additional applications to compare opinions and achieve consensus.

In some cases, the proposals will be read only by agency staff members rather than undergoing the peer review process described above. Government staffers may be more experienced at this and able to work more quickly, and the number of proposals may be relatively few in many instances. But they may also skim to save time.

What all this means is that, too often, proposals are never read word-for-word in their entirety. Of course any proposal *may* be studied thoroughly by one or more readers, and even with those who skim you can never be sure which portions will be read more completely. So you must do your best possible job on every page and every paragraph. Reviewers may form opinions quickly and perhaps inaccurately, missing key points in your application unless you take special measures to organize the proposal effectively.

Keeping in mind the way proposals may be read, the smart approach is to take the following steps:

1. *Use "white space" freely.* Assuming rigid length constraints do not prevent it, a good practice is arranging the text of your proposal with lots of white space (that is, space on the printed page that is not filled with type) to facilitate quick, easy reading. This can be accomplished by:

- Double-spacing (unless single-spacing is specifically mandated)
- Using wide margins (1 to 2 in)
- Presenting selected information in a list format rather than packing it into dense paragraphs, just as this list of tips is presented here
- Breaking the proposal into sections with clearly identified headings

and subheadings (and with liberal spacing above and below each heading)

2. *Highlight key points.* To make certain readers do not miss them, highlight key phrases by underlining them or printing them in boldface. If done consistently throughout the proposal, this can help guide readers through the application while emphasizing the points you consider most important.

3. *Use intentional repetition.* You may have been taught in English classes to avoid repeating yourself in written works. While this may be a basic principle of effective writing, the grant-writing process sometimes means steering away from conventional practices. In this case, repeating yourself is not a mistake; in fact, just the opposite is true.

Why? In scanning through a proposal, a reader may fail to see or fully absorb an important fact or explanation. Your proposal could even have points deducted for a lack of information when the material is actually covered adequately. Repeating key information can help prevent this from happening, if you observe these limitations:

- Spread information throughout the proposal. Repeating the same idea two or three times in close proximity can hurt more than help.
- Vary wording so that a point which is being reemphasized sounds slightly different in each instance.
- Use transitional phrases to avoid insulting the diligent reader's intelligence. For example, use phrases such as "as noted earlier" or "as pointed out in the need statement" to lead into statements containing repeated information.

4. *Add visual enhancements.* The old advice that "a picture is worth a thousand words" can be adapted to your advantage in developing competitive proposals. But instead of pictures, uses charts, graphs, or other visual enhancements to help readers understand what you are proposing. Examples of such material include:

- A flowchart illustrating a process that the project will accomplish
- A time line table (see Table 5-1)
- A bar graph detailing statistics used to support the need statement
- A chart illustrating an evaluation design (see Figure 5-1)
- A chart comparing data from one year to another

Such items need not be fancy; in fact, anything which is too elaborate

Table 5-1. Sample Timeline Table

Date	Develop inventory	Administer inventory	Advise clients	Sponsor special activities	Evaluate results (formative)	Evaluate results (summative)	Disseminate results
Oct–Nov 1991	X				X		
Dec–Jan 1991–92	X	X (test)			X		
Feb–March 1992	X				X		
Apr–May 1992	X				X		
June–July 1992		X	X		X		
Aug–Sept 1992		X	X		X	X	
Oct–Nov 1992			X	X	X		
Dec–Jan 1992–93		X	X	X	X		
Feb–Mar 1993	X*		X	X	X		
Apr–May 1993			X	X	X		
June–July 1993		X			X		
Aug–Sept 1993		X	X		X	X	
Oct–Nov 1993			X	X	X		
Dec–Jan 1993–94		X	X		X		
Feb–Mar 1994	X*		X	X	X		
Apr–May 1994			X	X	X		
June–July 1994		X			X		
Aug–Sept 1994		X	X	X	X	X	X

*Review of instrument with assistance of outside expert and improvements as needed.

PROPOSED EVALUATION COMPONENTS

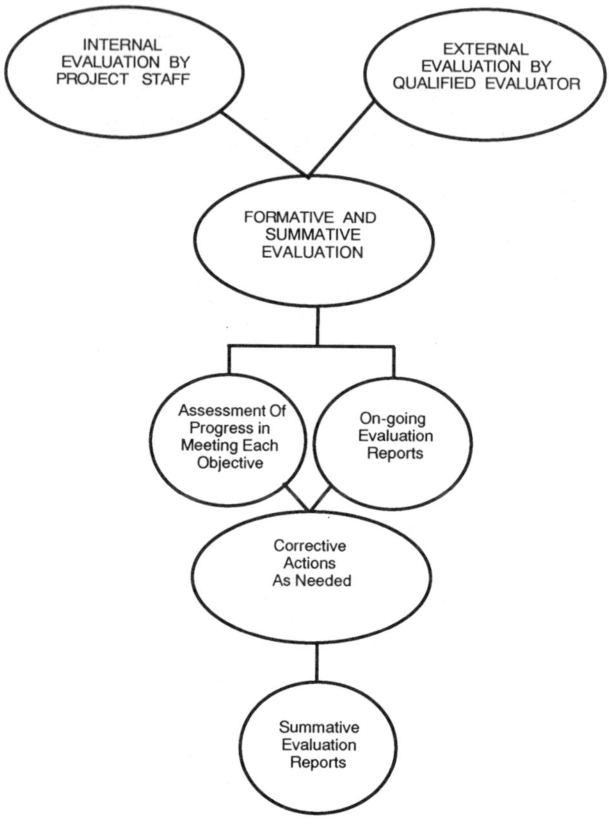

Figure 5-1. Sample chart illustrating evaluation design.

may be confusing or may come across as a gimmick. The main requirements are clarity and neatness. With the desktop publishing capabilities provided by many computer systems, developing these enhancements can often be accomplished quickly and easily.

Adding Finishing Touches

After making any necessary revisions or additions, make sure to take care of final details such as these:

1. *Proofread one last time.* A final review is vital. You might be surprised at the kinds of mistakes that can be overlooked through one or

more drafts. Read thoroughly and watch for grammatical or spelling errors, sloppy sentence construction, vagueness, or any other problems. Perfection might not be possible, but try to get close to it.

2. *Add pagination.* Since revisions may throw off sequencing, it is best to add page numbers as one of the last steps in the proposal revision process. But don't overlook the fact that every page in the proposal should have a page number. This will make copying easier and also helps guard against problems should one or more pages become separated from the application during the review process. Having a number for each page also comes in handy during telephone discussions and other communications about the proposal.

Unless otherwise directed, the best approach is to number pages consecutively from the cover sheet through any appendixes or forms. For example, in a 31-page proposal, numbers might be assigned as follows: page 1 for the title page or cover sheet, page 2 for the abstract, pages 3 to 15 for the narrative, pages 16 to 20 for the budget and budget attachments, 21 to 24 for the assurances, and 25 through 31 for appendixes.

Sometimes, other methods of designating page numbers will be preferred. If this is the case, the directions for completing the application will include instructions for pagination.

3. *Add an acknowledgment card.* Application packets often include a postcard, designed as a self-mailer, printed on the back cover of the booklet of forms and directions. This proposal acknowledgment card is used to notify the applicant that the proposal has been received by the funding agency. It also provides the applicant with a proposal number which should be used in any future correspondence or other communication about the proposal.

Filling out the card is simple. All you need do is write or type your name and address on the front side of the card and include the card with your proposal. Government staff members will fill out the reverse side and mail it to you after the proposal has been received. What may be more difficult, though, is simply remembering to include the card with your proposal. This is one of the most frequently overlooked steps in proposal completion, since it is usually done as one of the last tasks and may get lost in the effort to meet the deadline and prepare the proposal for mailing or delivery. To avoid this problem, be sure to complete the card early in the process and place it with your envelope or mailing labels.

4. *Use a proposal checklist.* Some proposals include a checklist for your use in proposal completion. If this is not provided, it is a good idea to make up your own or to adapt one from a different proposal. Following a checklist can help you avoid overlooking a key component of

Table 5.2. Sample Checklist for Proposal Preparation

INSTRUCTIONS: Please assemble your proposal in the following order. Required forms are included in this announcement and may be photocopied. Make sure to make sufficient copies for submission for continuation awards (continuation funding).

______	1. Federal Assistance Application (SF 424) Attached
______	2. Abstract
______	3. Budget (Form EIA-459C) Attached
______	4. Budget Explanation
______	5. Narrative
______	6. Vita for Project Director and Staff
______	7. Assurance of Compliance (DOE F 1600.5) Attached
______	8. Summary of Non-DOE Support Attached
______	9. Certification Regarding Drug-Free Workplace Requirements
______	10. Certification Regarding Disbarment, Suspension, and Other Responsibility Matters—Primary Covered Transaction
______	11. *6 copies* of the proposal including the signature copy.

the proposal. Table 5-2 is a checklist included with a grant package provided by the Department of Energy.

Taking Advantage of Word Processing

Any advice about proposal development and submission should include a few words about word processing. In the "old days," 10 or 15 years ago, grant and contract proposals were prepared with typewriters. But in today's world of rapid information processing, the only smart way to undertake proposal development is to use word processing.

Word processing might involve the use of any of the following:

- A computer which is used for a number of applications, one of which is the preparation of correspondence and manuscripts with word processing software
- A dedicated word processor used only for preparing manuscripts and correspondence
- A "smart" typewriter which has been enhanced so that it can store information electronically

Any of these is vastly superior to a traditional typewriter. No matter how limited your budget, make sure you beg, borrow, or otherwise gain access to word processing before starting the complex proposal development. If your business is a very small one, the actual process of keying in and manipulating information may be work which you will take on yourself. If not, this will be the responsibility of a secretary.

In either case, word processing is a key element in efficient proposal writing. It saves time and allows anyone, whether a highly skilled typist or the two-fingered, hunt-and-peck specialist, the luxury of making unlimited mistakes and then correcting them before they appear on paper. Each word, sentence, or paragraph can be corrected, deleted, moved, or otherwise manipulated until the writer is satisfied that it represents his or her best possible work.

No matter how fast you or your secretary types, the job can be completed more rapidly with word processing—a substantial element to consider in preparing long, complex proposals. (Much of this savings in time is due to the nature of the computer keyboard; there is no delay for mechanical processes such as movement from one line to the next or a key striking the paper or a typing element rotating.)

A computer saves you even more time because it allows you to revise and then revise again without retyping material. You can develop a first draft quickly, then review and expand it by inserting material without rekeying anything that is already there. Some writers develop a rough working outline and then follow up by inserting blocks of material under each subheading until the task is completed. At the same time, there is no need to work sequentially. In other words, the writer can work on any section of the proposal at any time rather than starting with the introductory portion and progressing through the other sections of the application. This allows more flexibility than would otherwise be possible; you can work on the section for which you have the most material, or simply on the section that strikes your fancy at the moment.

Another advantage of word processors and computers is the spell-checking programs available with many word processing software packages. This allows even the worst speller (and many intelligent people are not particularly good spellers) to submit materials with confidence that their efforts are not weakened by spelling errors.

A special boon of word processing is the capacity to produce a completely new proposal by editing one which has been stored on a disk or otherwise electronically retained. If you are truly interested in pursuing grants or contracts, then developing a single proposal will not be enough. You will want to prepare multiple applications for submission to other agencies or programs. This not only multiplies your chances of receiving an award but makes the initial investment of time in writing a proposal more cost-effective.

Meeting Submission Deadlines

The word *deadline* often carries a negative connotation, hinting of the stress which can be associated with rushing against the clock to complete a task by a specified date. Nevertheless, deadlines go hand in hand with grants and contracts. Most announcements of competitions for grants or contracts include a date by which they must be received. These deadlines are extremely important. In most cases, *a proposal which does not meet the published deadline will not be considered for funding.* It doesn't matter if you have a reasonable excuse or if your proposal is far better than all the others or if you apologize, threaten, or beg. Late proposals will be thrown out of the competition.

The definition of what is considered "on time" varies. Sometimes, the announced deadline represents when the proposal must be *received* by the funding agency. Other times, the deadline refers to the date by which the proposal has to be *mailed* or otherwise transmitted by the applicant; if the proposal is sent by this date, it is considered to be on time, even if it takes several days of transit time in the mail. The application announcement or guidelines will state the deadline and explain how to meet it.

Moreover, you must not just meet a deadline, you must *prove* that you have met it. Say, for example, that the U.S. Department of Education has a deadline of October 31, and the program guidelines say that any proposal mailed on or before that date will be considered. The department will accept any of the following as proof of mailing:

- A legibly dated U.S. Postal Service postmark
- A legible mail receipt with the date of mailing stamped by the U.S. Postal Service
- A date shipping label, invoice, or receipt from a commercial carrier
- Any other proof of mailing acceptable to the Department of Education

The Department will *not* accept the following:

- A privately metered postmark if the application is sent via the U.S. Postal Service
- A mail receipt that is not dated by the U.S. Postal Service

The Department of Education will also accept proposals which are delivered by hand or courier, as long as they arrive by the closing date and between 8:00 AM and 4:30 PM (Washington, DC, time).

Other federal agencies have similar practices, with all such provisions explained in instructions for application transmittal.

In meeting deadlines, try to follow these steps:

1. Write down or post the deadline for any program for which you plan to apply and keep it in a conspicuous place.
2. Plan the proposal development process with deadlines in mind.
3. Allow some time for contingencies (for example, what if it's 3:30 PM on the due date, and your photocopier breaks down?).
4. Obtain mailing labels, packaging, and so forth in advance.
5. If you use the U.S. Postal Service, have a postal worker postmark your package (or at least your receipt) before it leaves your hands. The Postal Service does not uniformly provide a dated postmark, and if you dropped off the package, it might lay around until after midnight and then receive a postmark for the following date.
6. Use registered or certified mail if possible, at least first-class mail.
7. If you use an overnight express service, be sure to obtain a dated receipt.
8. Whether you use the U.S. Postal Service or a private company, keep a dated receipt where it will not be misplaced and can easily be retrieved. A good place is stapled to the cover sheet of a file copy of your proposal.

Managing the Proposal Submission Process

Because of the volume of work required and the restrictions created by deadlines, developing proposals can be an exhausting process. The best way to approach such an effort is to develop a plan of action with self-imposed deadlines for completion of various portions or drafts of the proposal.

For example, if a proposal is due March 1, plan to have a rough draft completed by February 15 and a more polished version by February 25. That way, you can negotiate any roadblocks which pop up unexpectedly.

It is a good idea always to remember Murphy's Law ("what can go wrong, will") when planning and carrying out the proposal development process. If you plan ahead and allow yourself sufficient time to complete the various tasks involved, you can meet those deadlines with time to spare.

6
Budget Basics

Developing budgets is a routine function for most business operations, so this aspect of grant or contract development may seem more familiar to most people than some other steps in the application process. At the same time, it is important to realize that such budgets require special attention as one of the most important elements of any proposal.

In fact, quite often the budget section of a proposal serves as the core around which everything else is built. While the project narrative plays the greatest part in describing the proposed project, the budget determines exactly what will be undertaken. Without the dollars needed to carry out any activity, the narrative becomes little more than empty words.

In addition to the role a budget plays in the implementation of any program, the budget portion of a proposal may itself help determine whether a project is funded. In many cases, proposal reviewers assign point totals for the budget just as they would for other components of the application. A well-prepared budget earns vital support for the overall merits of the application. Conversely, a poorly prepared budget can lose points and, in a tightly competitive situation, prevent an application from being funded. Readers assess budgets by considering factors such as:

- The degree to which the budget is adequate for achieving the proposed goals and objectives
- The extent to which it is cost-effective
- The degree to which information is sufficient to judge the two factors listed above

Purpose

The purpose of a budget is to provide a written plan of expenditures proposed for a project. Just as in other types of budgets, those for government-funded projects usually are considered as guidelines rather than rigid boundaries, at least in the proposal stage. They are subject to change as awards are made and projects become more concrete.

Once a budget has been finalized, however, it becomes much less flexible. Changes may be hard to make, often requiring special approvals, and government policies and laws controlling financial transactions must be strictly followed.

Budgets can serve a number of functions:

- They allow readers to see exactly what you are proposing from a dollars-and-cents angle.
- They may keep projects from being overly ambitious by establishing a ceiling for spending.
- They can help reviewers compare the merits of proposals (especially in competitions for contracts, where cost may be the basis on which awards are made).
- They may serve as the basis for negotiation in the award process.
- They become the guide for implementation of funded projects.

Elements of a Proposed Budget

Formats for budgets presented in grant and contract proposals vary widely, but most contain certain basic components. Here is an overview of typical elements of a proposed budget.

Personnel

Any staff who will be funded through a proposed grant or contract project will be listed in the personnel section of the budget. This might consist of new staff who will be hired for the specific purpose of carrying out project activities. Or it might include existing staff who will be assigned to work on the project. Positions might be full-time, part-time, or a combination of the two.

The position most commonly listed in the personnel section of a proposal is that of project director. This is the person who will manage the project. The project director is responsible for carrying out the tasks proposed or supervising such work performed by others. Another major duty is seeing that all funds are expended in accordance with government guidelines, as well as filing any required reports.

The position of project director may be full-time, with 100 percent of duties being performed under the proposed project, or it may be a part-time role. For the latter, a staff member may be relieved of a portion of his or her regular duties for the duration of the project. For instance, this might consist of spending half of the work week in directing the project and the remaining time performing tasks totally unrelated to the grant or contract.

In the small business setting, this position may be undertaken by the person who owns the business or is one of its partners. In other words, you can put yourself down as project director if you so choose. As long as you would actually be able to take on the project for the amount of time proposed, there is no problem.

When listing personnel, a prime consideration is the amount to request for salaries. In general, government agencies will not stipulate salary levels but instead will allow the applicant to set them, within reasonable limits. The expectation is that the application follow the normal salary structure for other positions within the organization that are not funded by grants. In other words, you can't take advantage of the government to set up a grossly inflated salary for yourself or other project staff, but you can see that salaries are consistent with others in your firm or similar organizations.

In developing the personnel section of a budget, be sure to keep in mind the following:

1. The more dollars assigned to salaries, the less room for other expenditures in projects with an overall limitation on the size of the budget.
2. Winning funds for personnel can bring problems along with opportunities. For example, what happens when the grant period ends? You will need to find other funding for project staff or else be faced with terminating them.
3. With funds for personnel comes the obligation to use them for that purpose. If a grant covers 50 percent of a staff member's salary, for instance, you can't ask that individual to perform other duties during the time paid for by the grant or contract.
4. If you use government funds to hire personnel, you will need to take care to provide equal opportunities for minorities and other groups targeted by affirmative action and other policies.

Fringe Benefits

For any personnel costs, appropriate fringe benefit costs should be listed. Generally, the government will not stipulate the amount or percentage of fringe benefits to be provided, leaving that to the applicant. The expectation is that such costs be consistent with your normal policies for employees not being paid with grant funds and that such costs be reasonable in comparison with normal business standards.

For example, if a grant will pay for a project director with a salary of $40,000, you should take your standard benefit rate (say 30 percent), multiply the salary by this figure, and list the result ($12,000). For a part-time position that does not earn full benefits, those benefits involved should be similarly listed.

Somewhere in the budget, either on a space provided or on an attached sheet, be sure to break out fringe benefit costs and explain how they were calculated. Once this is done for one proposal, it can become boilerplate which can be added to other proposals with a minimum of effort.

Travel

Travel costs may or may not be included in a grant or contract budget. If included, such funds must be used only for travel that is directly related to achieving the goals set up for the project. For example, the project director may plan to attend a meeting in Washington, DC, to be held for all directors of similar projects (if so, this will probably be mentioned in the budget instructions). Or project staff may need to visit a university in another state to confer with a researcher who is an expert in a field related to the work being proposed.

Travel costs apply only to project staff, at least in this section of most budgets. Such costs as travel for consultants who are not staff members per se, or freight costs, are normally covered in the "Other" category described below.

It is important to be as specific as possible when providing budget details in this category. Proposal reviewers must be presented with enough information so that they (1) will understand why the proposed travel is necessary and (2) won't think too much money is being requested for any trips proposed. Budget forms rarely have sufficient space for this kind of detail, but you can provide it on an attachment as described later.

Foreign travel usually is not an allowable cost under most federal programs, except for those projects with an international basis where this is deemed necessary to project success.

If travel is included, it can be one of the more attractive features of receiving government funding. This may be especially true for small businesses where funds for travel are limited.

Equipment

Federal programs often support the acquisition of equipment deemed necessary to complete funded projects. Some programs place a major focus on equipment, having goals of updating equipment for scientific research or other purposes. Many others place less emphasis on equipment, but will approve it as a part of the overall funding package.

Before including equipment in the budget, check guidelines carefully to make certain this is allowable under the program for which you are applying. Then stay within any restrictions listed for amount or type of equipment.

The budget form may have space only for the total amount of funds to be expended, but additional details will be expected. The usual procedure is to break out each separate item of equipment that costs more than a specified amount (such as $500) on a separate sheet of paper, grouping together items costing less than this amount. The listing for each item should include a brief description which includes the name of the piece, the minimum configuration, and why it is needed. Brand names may be omitted, especially if competitive bidding is to be utilized which would preclude advance arrangements with any vendor or equipment supplier.

Supplies

In this section, supplies necessary for project support will be listed. These could range from laboratory supplies needed in a research project to ordinary office supplies used for project administration.

All supplies should be listed in sufficient detail to make their purpose and cost clear. Lab supplies, for example, should be broken down by type, quantity, and cost. Office supplies, on the other hand, could be designated as such without further explanation, as long as the amount requested is not unusually high (say no more than $500 for most programs).

Contractual Agreements

Any contractual agreements with other businesses or other organizations covered by project funds should be listed here. For example, a subcontract for the processing of survey forms might be included.

The actual agreements themselves should not be finalized until *after* the project has been funded; government requirements for bidding may need to be followed. At this stage, information on contractual agreements should be considered an estimate.

Contracts for individual consultants are not usually included in this section but instead are listed under Other as noted below.

Other Items

The Other category is used to cover items which do not fit readily under the standard budget headings. Examples of such costs include freight costs; telephone or other communications costs; rental rather than purchase of equipment; and computer use and consultant costs, including fees and travel for the consulting assignment. All costs under Other should be itemized.

Direct and Indirect Costs

The total of all costs in the categories discussed above will be the direct cost for the project. Most applications have at least one space where this total figure must be listed.

In addition, many agencies will support indirect costs associated with the project. These are the "hidden" costs incurred with any activity, which may not be reflected in the budget. For example, utilities and space usage may cost your firm money, even though such costs are not covered by project funds. Or an accountant on your staff may help keep track of project funds even though no direct costs for "accounting" are shown in the budget.

If possible, always build such costs into your proposal. These extra funds can make the difference in whether a project is profitable.

To calculate indirect costs, multiply the total direct cost by whatever percentage is allowed for the program under which funds are requested. This might be a standard figure (such as 8 percent) or a figure arrived at for your company after negotiation with government officials. In some cases, no indirect costs will be supported. In others, a substantial amount is possible. To find out which is the case, read budget instructions closely, and if necessary, contact program officials for a clarification. If indirect costs are allowed, be sure to list them in the appropriate budget space.

Matching Costs

Some grant programs require the grantee to cover a portion of costs needed to conduct the project. This varies from one program to another in terms of the amount needed (if any) and what will be acceptable as a matching contribution.

If matching requirements are mentioned in application materials, be sure to study them carefully and consider whether your firm would be willing to provide them if the project is funded.

Tips for Budget Development

In putting together a budget for a grant or contact proposal, it will help to follow these tips:

1. *Always double-check your budget figures.* Largely as a result of the pressures of impending deadlines, budgets presented in proposals too often contain mathematical mistakes, omissions, or other errors. Such mistakes can be doubly troublesome. If noticed by a reviewer, they can cause you to lose points in the proposal review process. And even if not noticed at this stage, mistakes can cause substantial problems if a project is funded. A simple addition or multiplication error, for instance, can leave the project $10,000 short of the funds necessary to carry out an activity proposed in the application.

To avoid errors, check your figures after they have been calculated and again after they have been typed. Use a calculator to recheck each item. Many budget forms have both horizontal rows and vertical columns. Totaling your budget in each of these rows and columns will ensure overall accuracy.

If possible, ask someone else to duplicate this checking process to make sure you have not overlooked anything. As with the old adage about not seeing the forest for the trees, sometimes the person who originally prepares a budget can be too close to it to notice flaws. Anyone who is handy with a calculator can help in this manner, whether a secretary, a helpful spouse, or a staff member who works with financial transactions.

2. *Don't save budget preparation until last.* In some proposals, the budget section is presented at or near the back of the application. As a result, the tendency is to finish the rest of the proposal before tackling the budget. But this can be a mistake for several reasons.

First, completing the budget helps in making decisions which will have an effect on the rest of the proposal. For example, say that a grant competition specifies a maximum award of $50,000. That is a large amount of money in one sense, but it also may be significantly less than the amount you would like to have for addressing a particular topic. But building a budget early in the proposal development process will force you to keep costs within the guidelines and then develop strategies which match those cost levels. This may mean limiting personnel commitments, deciding not to ask for a given piece of equipment, or similar actions. In any case, it is much less trouble to discover your financial limits early rather than after you have developed the proposal, overshot the budget and then had to delete much of what you had written. Even if deletions are not necessary, making early budget decisions helps crystallize your thinking.

Second, waiting until the last minute to complete the budget invites errors. The nature of grant and contract deadlines often leads to some hurried work. This may be inevitable at least some of the time, but it is unwise to hurry in developing budget information. Unless you are a math whiz, the result can range from calculation errors to the presentation of contradictory information. And an error in subtraction, addition, multiplication, or calculating a percentage can have a disastrous cumulative effect, causing mistakes throughout your budget. The better alternative is to start early and work methodically on this section of the application.

3. *Understand budget evaluation criteria.* Reviewers will ask themselves whether your budget follows the priorities established for the program under which funds are being sought. In most cases, they will look at a list of criteria for the budget which has been included in the application materials. Since you also have access to this information, it is wise to study these details and then construct your budget accordingly.

4. *Be reasonable.* Everyone has heard of $100 bolts and other excesses sometimes occurring in projects funded by the government. But don't assume that you can take advantage of government agencies in this way. Building in excess costs may earn you low ratings and prevent your project from being funded. To avoid such problems, be sure that all costs included in the budget would seem reasonable to an objective reader.

5. *Duplicate extra forms.* Before filling out budget forms, be sure to make several photocopies of each form. This will allow you to write a first draft on one set of forms while saving another for the final, typed draft. Having extra forms will also allow you to cope if extensive corrections must be made and retyping becomes necessary.

6. *Relate each budget item to the rest of the proposal.* Nothing should appear in the budget which does not relate directly to information discussed elsewhere in the application. Once a budget has been developed in draft form, look at each item and make sure it is explained in the project narrative.

7. *If in doubt, explain.* If it is not readily understandable why an item appears as it does, take the time to explain your rationale. Too much information in the budget is almost always better than too little; reviewers do not like to guess about budget details.

This is most effectively done by using budget attachments. Once completed, budget forms provide a basic overview, but they do not necessarily tell the whole story. Reviewers and program staff often want to know more details about items and amounts listed in the budget. For instance, a total figure may be given for fringe benefits, but the form does not leave room to show how this figure was calculated. Or a figure for Other will give no clue as to what is actually being requested.

The solution? Simply attach extra pages detailing such information, perhaps under the heading "Additional Budget Information." Here are some examples:

- Under fringe benefits (item 2 on the budget page), a total figure is listed in the summary budget of $8,376. In the attachment, it is broken out as shown below:

Item 2: *Fringe Benefits*

Calculated at 30% as follows:	
Retirement	8.00%
Social Security	7.62%
Health insurance	10.20%
Worker's Compensation Insurance	2.10%
Overall benefits	
	27.92%
27.92% × $30,000 = $8,376	

- Under travel, a total of $910 is listed. This is explained as follows:

Attendance at conference, "Computer Applications for the Learning Disabled Student," May 11–12 in Chicago, Ill.	
Registration fee	$295
Hotel	180
Commercial airfare	345
Ground transportation	30
Per diem at $30	60
Total	
	$900

Similar details can be added about equipment, supplies, or other items.

8. *Utilize highlighting and effective spacing.* Just as in the written narrative, in the budget it is in your best interest to make information as

clear and easy to read as possible. Use underlining, boldface, or spacing to emphasize key points.

9. *Make sure all budget pages are identified and numbered.* Readers sometimes remove budget pages from a proposal to work with them separately or to make comparisons with other sections. To ensure that budget pages or attachments are not misplaced, number each one and include in the heading the name of your project or your company name.

Filling Out Budget Forms

Most applications include special forms for the budget. These may appear imposing, but they are often less difficult to complete than you might think. Sample budget forms are provided as Figs. 6-1, 6-2, 6-3, and 6-4.

Most budget forms include detailed instructions for completion. Just take your time and read the instructions carefully before filling in figures, and even without prior experience you should be able to do a credible job.

In some instances, budget forms may not be provided. In this case, it is acceptable to devise your own format. The easiest approach is simply to list several budget categories and then fill in information as you see fit. As with preprinted forms, the main factor is to include sufficient detail, with explanations where warranted.

Sometimes you will be requested to provide a brief overview of the budget in the project narrative, with full details covered in the forms. If this is the case, be sure to check these sections against each other to ensure total consistency.

Overall Requirements

Any grant or contract budget must meet the following requirements:

1. All costs must be reasonable.
2. All costs must be necessary to accomplish project objectives.
3. Costs must be allowable in terms of the applicable federal cost principles.
4. All financial transactions must be auditable.
5. All costs must be incurred within the designated period of project funding.

If these requirements are met and care is taken to fully explain all information, your budget can be highly effective.

OMB Approval No. 0348-0044

BUDGET INFORMATION — Non-Construction Programs

SECTION A – BUDGET SUMMARY

Grant Program Function or Activity (a)	Catalog of Federal Domestic Assistance Number (b)	Estimated Unobligated Funds		New or Revised Budget		
		Federal (c)	Non-Federal (d)	Federal (e)	Non-Federal (f)	Total (g)
1.		$	$	$	$	$
2.						
3.						
4.						
5. TOTALS		$	$	$	$	$

SECTION B – BUDGET CATEGORIES

6 Object Class Categories	GRANT PROGRAM, FUNCTION OR ACTIVITY				Total (5)
	(1)	(2)	(3)	(4)	
a. Personnel	$	$	$	$	$
b. Fringe Benefits					
c. Travel					
d. Equipment					
e. Supplies					
f. Contractual					
g. Construction					
h. Other					
i. Total Direct Charges (sum of 6a - 6h)					
j. Indirect Charges					
k. TOTALS (sum of 6i and 6j)	$	$	$	$	$
7. Program Income	$	$	$	$	$

Authorized for Local Reproduction

Standard Form 424A (4-88)
Prescribed by OMB Circular A-102

Figure 6-1. Sample budget form, U.S. Department of Education.

SECTION C - NON-FEDERAL RESOURCES

(a) Grant Program	(b) Applicant	(c) State	(d) Other Sources	(e) TOTALS
8.	$	$	$	$
9.				
10.				
11.				
12. TOTALS (sum of lines 8 and 11)	$	$	$	$

SECTION D - FORECASTED CASH NEEDS

	Total for 1st Year	1st Quarter	2nd Quarter	3rd Quarter	4th Quarter
13. Federal	$	$	$	$	$
14. NonFederal					
15. TOTAL (sum of lines 13 and 14)	$	$	$	$	$

SECTION E - BUDGET ESTIMATES OF FEDERAL FUNDS NEEDED FOR BALANCE OF THE PROJECT

(a) Grant Program	FUTURE FUNDING PERIODS (Years)			
	(b) First	(c) Second	(d) Third	(e) Fourth
16.	$	$	$	$
17.				
18.				
19.				
20. TOTALS (sum of lines 16-19)	$	$	$	$

SECTION F - OTHER BUDGET INFORMATION

(Attach additional Sheets if Necessary)

21. Direct Charges:	22. Indirect Charges:
23. Remarks	

SF 424A (4-88) Page 2
Prescribed by OMB Circular A-102

Authorized for Local Reproduction

Figure 6-1 *(Continued)*

INSTRUCTIONS FOR THE SF-424A

General Instructions

This form is designed so that application can be made for funds from one or more grant programs. In preparing the budget, adhere to any existing Federal grantor agency guidelines which prescribe how and whether budgeted amounts should be separately shown for different functions or activities within the program. For some programs, grantor agencies may require budgets to be separately shown by function or activity. For other programs, grantor agencies may require a breakdown by function or activity. Sections A,B,C, and D should include budget estimates for the whole project except when applying for assistance which requires Federal authorization in annual or other funding period increments. In the latter case, Sections A,B, C, and D should provide the budget for the first budget period (usually a year) and Section E should present the need for Federal assistance in the subsequent budget periods. All applications should contain a breakdown by the object class categories shown in Lines a-k of Section B.

Section A. Budget Summary
Lines 1-4, Columns (a) and (b)

For applications pertaining to a *single* Federal grant program (Federal Domestic Assistance Catalog number) and *not requiring* a functional or activity breakdown, enter on Line 1 under Column (a) the catalog program title and the catalog number in Column (b).

For applications pertaining to a *single* program *requiring* budget amounts by multiple functions or activities, enter the name of each activity or function on each line in Column (a), and enter the catalog number in Column (b). For applications pertaining to multiple programs where none of the programs require a breakdown by function or activity, enter the catalog program title on each line in *Column* (a) and the respective catalog number on each line in Column (b).

For applications pertaining to *multiple* programs where one or more programs *require* a breakdown by function or activity, prepare a separate sheet for each program requiring the breakdown. Additional sheets should be used when one form does not provide adequate space for all breakdown of data required. However, when more than one sheet is used, the first page should provide the summary totals by programs.

Lines 1-4, Columns (c) through (g.)

For new applications, leave Columns (c) and (d) blank. For each line entry in Columns (a) and (b), enter in Columns (e), (f), and (g) the appropriate amounts of funds needed to support the project for the first funding period (usually a year).

Lines 1-4, Columns (c) through (g.) (continued)

For continuing grant program applications, submi these forms before the end of each funding period a: required by the grantor agency. Enter in Columns (c and (d) the estimated amounts of funds which wil remain unobligated at the end of the grant fundin; period only if the Federal grantor agency instruction: provide for this. Otherwise, leave these column: blank. Enter in columns (e) and (f) the amounts o funds needed for the upcoming period. The amount(s in Column (g) should be the sum of amounts ir Columns (e) and (f).

For supplemental grants and changes to existin; grants, do not use Columns (c) and (d). Enter ir Column (e) the amount of the increase or decrease o Federal funds and enter in Column (f) the amount o the increase or decrease of non-Federal funds. Ir Column (g) enter the new total budgeted amoun (Federal and non-Federal) which includes the tota previous authorized budgeted amounts plus or minus as appropriate, the amounts shown in Columns (e) an((f). The amount(s) in Column (g) should not equal th(sum of amounts in Columns (e) and (f).

Line 5 — Show the totals for all columns used.

Section B Budget Categories

In the column headings (1) through (4), enter the title of the same programs, functions, and activities showi on Lines 1-4, Column (a), Section A.. When additiona sheets are prepared for Section A, provide simila column headings on each sheet. For each program function or activity, fill in the total requirements fo funds (both Federal and non-Federal) by object clas categories.

Lines 6a-i — Show the totals of Lines 6a to 6h in eacl column.

Line 6j - Show the amount of indirect cost.

Line 6k - Enter the total of amounts on Lines 6i an(6j. For all applications for new grants an(continuation grants the total amount in column (5) Line 6k, should be the same as the total amount show: in Section A, Column (g), Line 5. For supplementa grants and changes to grants, the total amount of th increase or decrease as shown in Columns (1)-(4), Lin 6k should be the same as the sum of the amounts i. Section A, Columns (e) and (f) on Line 5.

SF 424A (4-88) page

Figure 6-2. Sample budget instructions, U.S. Department of Education.

INSTRUCTIONS FOR THE SF-424A *(continued)*

Line 7 - Enter the estimated amount of income, if any, expected to be generated from this project. Do not add or subtract this amount from the total project amount. Show under the program narrative statement the nature and source of income. The estimated amount of program income may be considered by the federal grantor agency in determining the total amount of the grant.

Section C. Non-Federal-Resources

Lines 8-11 - Enter amounts of non-Federal resources that will be used on the grant. If in-kind contributions are included, provide a brief explanation on a separate sheet.

> **Column (a)** - Enter the program titles identical to Column (a), Section A. A breakdown by function or activity is not necessary.
>
> **Column (b)** - Enter the contribution to be made by the applicant.
>
> **Column (c)** - Enter the amount of the State's cash and in-kind contribution if the applicant is not a State or State agency. Applicants which are a State or State agencies should leave this column blank.
>
> **Column (d)** - Enter the amount of cash and in-kind contributions to be made from all other sources.
>
> **Column (e)** - Enter totals of Columns (b), (c), and (d).

Line 12 — Enter the total for each of Columns (b)-(e). The amount in Column (e) should be equal to the amount on Line 5, Column (f), Section A.

Section D. Forecasted Cash Needs

Line 13 - Enter the amount of cash needed by quarter from the grantor agency during the first year.

Line 14 - Enter the amount of cash from all other sources needed by quarter during the first year.

Line 15 - Enter the totals of amounts on Lines 13 and 14.

Section E. Budget Estimates of Federal Funds Needed for Balance of the Project

Lines 16 - 19 - Enter in Column (a) the same grant program titles shown in Column (a), Section A. A breakdown by function or activity is not necessary. For new applications and continuation grant applications, enter in the proper columns amounts of Federal funds which will be needed to complete the program or project over the succeeding funding periods (usually in years). This section need not be completed for revisions (amendments, changes, or supplements) to funds for the current year of existing grants.

If more than four lines are needed to list the program titles, submit additional schedules as necessary.

Line 20 - Enter the total for each of the Columns (b)-(e). When additional schedules are prepared for this Section, annotate accordingly and show the overall totals on this line.

Section F. Other Budget Information

Line 21 - Use this space to explain amounts for individual direct object-class cost categories that may appear to be out of the ordinary or to explain the details as required by the Federal grantor agency.

Line 22 - Enter the type of indirect rate (provisional, predetermined, final or fixed) that will be in effect during the funding period, the estimated amount of the base to which the rate is applied, and the total indirect expense.

Line 23 - Provide any other explanations or comments deemed necessary.

Figure 6-2 *(Continued)*

(SEE INSTRUCTIONS ON REVERSE BEFORE COMPLETING

SUMMARY PROPOSAL BUDGET

	FOR NSF USE ONLY		
ORGANIZATION	PROPOSAL NO.	DURATION (MONTHS)	
		Proposed	Granted
PRINCIPAL INVESTIGATOR/PROJECT DIRECTOR	AWARD NO.		

A. SENIOR PERSONNEL: PI/PD. Co-PI's, Faculty and Other Senior Associates (List each separately with title, A.6. show number in brackets)	NSF Funded Person-mos. CAL.	ACAD	SUMR	Funds Requested By Proposer	Funds Granted By NSF (If Different)
1.				$	$
2.					
3.					
4.					
5. ( ) OTHERS (LIST INDIVIDUALLY ON BUDGET EXPLANATION PAGE)					
6. ( ) TOTAL SENIOR PERSONNEL (1-5)					
B. OTHER PERSONNEL (SHOW NUMBERS IN BRACKETS)					
1. ( ) POST DOCTORAL ASSOCIATES					
2. ( ) OTHER PROFESSIONALS (TECHNICIAN, PROGRAMMER, ETC.)					
3. ( ) GRADUATE STUDENTS					
4. ( ) UNDERGRADUATE STUDENTS					
5. ( ) SECRETARIAL CLERICAL					
6. ( ) OTHER					
TOTAL SALARIES AND WAGES (A+B)					
C. FRINGE BENEFITS (IF CHARGED AS DIRECT COSTS)					
TOTAL SALARAIES, WAGES AND FRINGE BENEFITS (A+B+C)					
D. PERMANENT EQUIPMENT (LIST ITEM AND DOLLAR AMOUNT FOR EACH ITEM EXCEEDING $1,000:)					
TOTAL PERMANENT EQUIPMENT					
E. TRAVEL 1. DOMESTIC (INCL. CANADA AND U.S. POSSESSIONS)					
2. FOREIGN					
F. PARTICIPANT SUPPORT COSTS 1. STIPENDS $ ______ 2. TRAVEL ______ 3. SUBSISTENCE ______ 4. OTHER ______					
( ) TOTAL PARTICIPANT COSTS					
G. OTHER DIRECT COSTS					
1. MATERIALS AND SUPPLIES					
2. PUBLICATION COSTS/DOCUMENTATION/DISSEMINATION					
3. CONSULTANT SERVICES					
4. COMPUTER (ADPE) SERVICES					
5. SUBCONTRACTS					
6. OTHER					
TOTAL OTHER DIRECT COSTS					
H. TOTAL DIRECT COSTS (A THROUGH G)					
I. INDIRECT COSTS (SPECIFY RATE AND BASE)					
TOTAL INDIRECT COSTS					
J. TOTAL DIRECT AND INDIRECT COSTS (H + I)					
K. RESIDUAL FUNDS (IF FOR FURTHER SUPPORT OF CURRENT PROJECTS SEE GPM 252 AND 253)					
L. AMOUNT OF THIS REQUEST (J) OR (J MINUS K)				$	$

PI/PD TYPED NAME & SIGNATURE*	DATE	FOR NSF USE ONLY		
		INDIRECT COST RATE VERIFICATION		
INST. REP. TYPED NAME & SIGNATURE*	DATE	Date Checked	Date of Rate Sheet	Inititals-DGC

NSF Form 1030 (8/90) *Supersedes All Previous Editions* *SIGNATURES REQUIRED ONLY FOR REVISED BUDGET (GPM 233)

Figure 6-3. Sample budget form, National Science Foundation.

INSTRUCTIONS FOR USE OF SUMMARY PROPOSAL BUDGET (NSF FORM 1030)

1. General

a. Each grant proposal, including requests for supplemental funding, must contain a Summary Proposal Budget in this format unless a pertinent program guideline specifically provides otherwise. A Summary Proposal Budget need not be submitted for incremental funding unless the original grant letter did not indicate specific incremental funding or if adjustments to the planned increment exceeding 10% or $10,000 are being requested.

b. Copies of NSF Form 1030 and instructions should be reproduced locally as NSF will not supply the form.

c. A separate form should be completed for each year of support requested. An additional form showing the cuculative budget for the full term requested should be completed for proposals requesting more than one year's support. Identify each year's request (e.g., "First year ________," or "Cumulative Budget," etc.) in the margin at the top right of the form.

d. Completion of this summary does not eliminate the need to fully document and justify the amounts requested in each category. Such documentation should be provided on additional page(s) immediately following the budget in the proposal and should be identified by line item. The documentation page(s) should be titled "Budget Explanation Page."

e. If a revised budget is required by NSF, it must be signed and dated by the Authorized Organizational Representative and Principal Investigator and submitted in at least the original and two copies.

2. Budget Line Items

A full discussion of the budget and the allowability of selected items of cost is contained in Grants for Research and Education in Science and Engineering, NSF Grant Policy Manual—GPM (NSF 88-47 periodically revised), and other NSF program brochures and guidelines. Following is a brief outline of budget documentation requirements by line item. (NOTE: All documentation or justification required on the line items below should be provided on the Budget Explanation Page.)

A., B., and C. Salaries, Wages, and Fringe Benefits (GPM 511 and GPM 205.1). On the Budget Explanation Page, list individually all senior personnel who were grouped under A5, the requested person-months to be funded, and rates of pay.

D. Permanent Equipment (GPM 512 and 204.2). While items exceeding $500 and 2 years' useful life are defined as permanent equipment, it is only necessary to list item and dollar amount for each item exceeding $1,000. Fully justify.

E. Travel (GPM 514 and GPM 730). Address the type and extent of travel (including consultant travel) and its relation to the project. Itemize by destination and cost and justify travel outside the United States and its possessions, Puerto Rico, and Canada. Include dates of foreign visits or meetings. Fare allowances are limited to round-trip, jet-economy rates.

F. Participant Support Costs (GPM 518). Normally participant support may only be requested for grants supporting conferences, workshops or symposia. Show number of participants in brackets. Consult Grants for Research and Education in Science and Engineering or specific program guidelines.

G. Other Direct Costs.

1. Materials and Supplies (GPM 513). Indicate types required and estimate costs.
2. Publication, Documentation, Dissemination (GPM 517). Estimate costs of documenting, preparing, publishing, disseminating, and sharing research findings.
3. Consultant Services (GPM 516). Indicate name, daily compensation (limited to GS-18 daily rate), and estimated days of service, and justify.
4. Computer Services (GPM 515). Include justification based on established computer service rates at the proposing institution. Purchase of equipment is included under D.
5. Subcontracts (GPM 623 and Exh. V-1). Include a complete budget and justify details.
6. Other. Itemize and justify. Include computer equipment leasing.

I. Indirect Costs (GPM 530). Specify current rate(s) and base(s). Use current rate(s) negotiated with the cognizant Federal negotiating agency. See GPM for special policy regarding grants to individuals, travel grants, equipment grants, doctoral dissertation grants, and grants involving participant support costs (chap. V, GPM).

K. Residual Funds (GPM 253). For incremental funding requests on continuing grants, enter the amount estimated to be in excess of 20% at the planned amendment effective date. If less than 20%, indicate: "none." Residual funds should not be reflected in budget categories A-I. A justification for carryover of funds in excess of 20% is required.

L. Item L will be the same as Item J unless the Foundation disapproves the carryover of funds. If disapproved, Item L will equal J minus K.

APPLICANTS MUST NOT ALTER OR REARRANGE THE COST CATEGORIES AS THEY APPEAR ON THIS FORM. WHICH IS DESIGNED FOR COMPATIBILITY WITH DATA CAPTURE BY NSF'S MANAGEMENT INFORMATION SYSTEM. IMPROPER COMPLETION OF THIS FORM MAY RESULT IN RETURN OF PROPOSAL TO APPLICANT.

Figure 6-4. Sample budget instructions, National Science Foundation.

7
Administering Funded Programs

A great deal of work may go into the development of a grant or contract proposal, but the work does not stop there. At least that's what you hope! If the proposal is not funded, your work will be finished for that particular competition. But if you actually win an award, a new set of tasks must be accomplished.

Of course, landing an award is the goal toward which you have been striving. As a businessperson, you probably feel some extra work is nothing to complain about. On the contrary, receiving a letter or phone call informing you that your project is being funded means a tremendous opportunity has become a reality for you and your company.

When the celebrating stops, you will need to set up the mechanisms for administering your project. Doing business with the government, as you may already realize, means that certain strings are attached. In accepting government funds, you also accept the responsibility of meeting government requirements for managing a project. This includes following certain rules for making financial transactions, completing regular reports to the funding agency, and in general operating the project in accordance with rules and regulations stipulated by the government.

If this sound onerous, don't worry. You can meet these requirements without hiring an army of attorneys or accountants. You simply must do the following:

1. Conduct the business set forth in your proposal (in other words, consider it as a contract which must be honored completely and diligently).
2. Do your best to meet all the established goals and objectives.

3. Stay within the official project period for all official activities.
4. Become familiar with government policies and laws regarding expenditure of funds.
5. Complete and maintain detailed documentation for all project activities.
6. Submit reports to the funding agency as required.

Accepting and Negotiating Awards

Learning that you have landed a government grant or contract can be one of life's sweetest moments. It's hard to top the satisfaction of knowing that your hard work in proposal development has paid off, not to mention the potential boost any award can provide to your small business.

An interesting factor here is the element of surprise. In many cases, weeks or months will pass between the time a proposal has been submitted and the day you learn it has been funded. The proposal may have been largely forgotten in the crush of day-to-day business. But then you receive notification of funding, and it may seem like Christmas or your birthday. This kind of delayed gratification can be a real pleasure.

Notification of funding may come in any one of a number of ways. You might receive a telephone call or fax message that your project has been recommended for funding. This almost always means it *will* be funded, but nothing is official until written confirmation follows. Or you might receive a letter stating essentially the same thing. The language may be cautiously bureaucratic, using phrasing such as "recommended for funding," "tentatively slated for funding," "tentatively approved" or the object of "intent to make an award" rather than a flat-out promise of funding. This protects the agency in case there are last-minute problems such as budget cuts at the agency or a problem with your proposed budget which cannot be resolved to the agency's satisfaction. But these problems are unlikely, and a preliminary notice almost always leads to the real thing.

Award notifications are not always made on a preliminary basis, however. You may receive a letter stating without reservation that your company is being awarded a grant or contract.

Once you do receive official notification, it will contain basic information such as the amount of the award, the applicable time period, and other details. A notice of award from the U.S. Department of Education, for instance, will include these details:

1. *Recipient name.* This will include the applicant's legal name and complete address.

2. *Project title.* This will be a brief description of the project as shown on the application form. The Catalog of Federal Domestic Assistance (CFDA) title of the overall program will also be listed, if applicable.

3. *Project staff.* Here, names and phone numbers will be listed for Department of Education staff members responsible for project direction and oversight. These are very important, for they are the persons whom you can contact with questions or problems. Often, two different persons will be listed—one responsible for programmatic concerns and the other for business and administrative matters. The local project director (that is, you or someone at your company designated to administer the project) will also be included.

4. *Award information.* Information identifying this unique project will be identified here. Especially important is a grant number assigned to this project. It should be used on all future correspondence related to the project to keep it from being identified mistakenly. Other details which might be listed include the type of award (such as discretionary grant) and action type (such as new award, continuation award, or revision of an existing grant).

5. *Award period.* Two types of award periods may be listed. The budget period is the time within which funds may be expended for this project. *This is critical information.* No financial transactions can take place before the beginning date listed or after the final date of the budget period. This needs to be clearly understood by anyone connected with the project.

A project period may also be listed which can be the same or longer than the budget period. A project can be planned for three years, for example, but each budget period may be limited to one 12-month period.

6. *Authorized funding.* This is the amount of money being funded. Figures might be expressed separately for the budget period and the project period. In addition, special circumstances may be detailed such as budget changes, funds authorized for carryover from one year to a subsequent year, and costs being shared by the recipient.

7. *Administrative information.* Details are provided here on how payments will be made and special regulations which must be followed.

In addition, a special number will be listed here to be used in financial transactions between your company and the agency.

8. *Legislative and fiscal data.* The federal law authorizing this grant or contract will be listed here along with related information.

9. *Terms and conditions of award.* This section notes any requirements not listed elsewhere which are binding on the recipient. The official authorized to award federal funds for this program will also be listed here.

All agencies do not provide identical information in award notices, but these kinds of details will normally be provided at least to some degree. Once you obtain the award notice, be sure to read and study the information carefully, and then file the award document where it will not be misplaced or forgotten (in fact, filing two or three copies in different files is a good precautionary measure).

Amending Budgets

In some cases, the award will be for exactly the amount presented in the proposal. In others, it will be for a different amount (usually less than you requested). In this event, an official of the approving agency may contact you to "negotiate" the award.

Say, for instance, that your proposed project budget was for $75,000, but the agency indicates it intends to make an award of $60,000. This frequently happens (especially with grants) because reviewers felt some of your proposed expenditures were unnecessary or because the agency wanted to make multiple awards and intended to distribute funds among a number of projects or for other reasons. In any case, this means your budget and the plan of action it supports must be amended. This amendment may be a one-way or a two-way process. In other words, you may be asked where you would prefer to have the budget reduced, or you may simply be told where the cuts will take place.

Sometimes, an agency official will telephone and discuss the budget with you, suggesting or directing types and amounts of changes. Even though this negotiation may be somewhat one-sided, at least it allows some discussion before the final award is set. In some instances, you may be able to convince the official to refrain from cutting certain items or to make adjustments in a different portion of the budget. In others, there is little recourse but to accept the mandated changes.

An alternative method sometimes allowed is to revise the budget in the way you see fit, send it in for approval, and then wait for approval from the funding agency. Using this approach you would decide where to cut the $15,000 from the project as originally proposed, and amend the budget accordingly.

In either case, the revised budget will become the standard against which your project must operate. So be cautious in working through this stage, and make certain you understand what is involved. The following steps can help in this process:

1. Keep a copy of your proposal handy in case an agency official calls to discuss it. This will prevent inconvenience or even the embarrassment of not being prepared to respond to questions or comments about the project.
2. Be deferential in dealing with agency staff. Remember, they are the givers and you are the recipient. You are not in a position to make demands or insist on anything.
3. Anytime you deal with an agency official by telephone, make a brief written record of the date, time, and substance of the conversation. This can be helpful if you get conflicting messages from different officials or simply need to clarify a point later.
4. Be prompt in providing requested revisions.
5. Once a budget has been revised, be sure to update all of the former versions in all file copies of your proposal. If this step is neglected, you could find yourself operating from two different budgets.

Implementing the Project

Once all changes are approved and you receive an official award notice, you can begin implementing your project. This should include some or all of the following steps:

1. Set up separate files for the project apart from others used for your business.

2. Develop a system for documenting all activities related to the project. Documentation is critical not only for routine management and reporting but if you are ever audited by the government. Examples of documents which should be maintained include:

- Purchase orders
- Payroll information, if applicable
- Time sheets or other work records
- Contractual agreements
- Information to show you have met affirmative action requirements

- Inventory records for equipment purchased with project funds
- All correspondence with government officials related to the project
- Progress reports
- Research records, if applicable
- Records of all financial transactions connected to the project
- Any other records suggested or required by the funding agency

3. Obtain information about administering your program. For any funded program, you should be able to obtain detailed regulations for project management. Such information tends to vary from one agency to the next. The Public Health Service, for example, maintains a detailed manual of policies which must be followed in administering funded programs. This manual may be consulted to determine exactly what actions are allowable in a given situation. The National Science Foundation not only offers the "NSF Grant Policy Manual" but also the publications "Grant General Conditions" and "Federal Demonstration Project General Terms and Conditions" for specific types of projects. Figure 7-1 is an example of an NSF policy statement.

In many cases, this kind of information will be provided when you receive funding. If it is not, check with agency officials to see what is available. Then once you obtain the information, follow the regulations carefully.

4. Stay on top of the project. As the project progresses, it is very important to maintain close control of the activities being undertaken. If you are the project director, set up a time line for accomplishment of major tasks, if this is not already provided in the proposal. Then make certain that activities are undertaken as promised.

If you are not the project director, make certain that the person directing the project reports frequently to you or another appropriate person in your firm.

A common problem in funded projects is to get behind on key tasks and then run out of time before the project is completed. The result can be funds left over which the government will not allow you to spend.

Making Changes in Funded Programs

Even in the most well-planned proposals, it is next to impossible to foresee every possible development which will occur during the implementation and completion of the project. It is not unusual to be faced with changes in the activities carried out or in the project budget.

WASHINGTON, DC 20550

GRANT POLICY MANUAL TRANSMITTAL MEMORANDUM NO. 2

February 20, 1990

Purpose. This memorandum provides guidance on the requirements of Section 1352, Title 31, U.S. Code, which limits the use of appropriated funds to influence certain Federal contracting and financial transactions.

Background/Summary of New Requirements. The new law, effective December 23, 1989, requires that before a grant, cooperative agreement or contract exceeding $100,000 can be awarded, the recipient must:

a) certify that no appropriated funds were or will be expended to pay any person for influencing or attempting to influence an officer or employee of any agency, a Member of Congress, an officer or employee of Congress, or an employee of a Member of Congress in connection with a specific award; and

b) disclose certain information if the recipient has used or intends to use non-appropriated funds to pay for the lobbying activities of an individual or organization not regularly employed by the applicant. Initial Disclosure Forms, if required, must be filed prior to award, and thereafter at the end of each calendar quarter in which there occurs any event that requires disclosure or that materially affects the accuracy of the information contained in any previously filed Disclosure Form.

The above certification and disclosure requirements apply to standard grant actions (new/renewals/supplements), cooperative agreements and contracts that exceed $100,000, and new continuing grants where the total multi-year support exceeds $100,000. It does not apply to scheduled increments for existing continuing grants, cooperative agreements and contracts that were awarded prior to December 23, 1989.

For any proposal that meets the threshhold defined above, certification should be made by grant applicants at the time of proposal submission, by attaching the full text certification (Attachment A) to the signed cover sheet. The certification text is attached as new page II-14c. The Disclosure Form will be available as a government Standard Form (currently carrying a dummy number SF-LLL, as shown in the December 20, 1989, issue of the Federal Register, Part VII). Grants for Research and Education in Science and Engineering, (NSF 83-57, October 1989) will also be revised to incorporate these new requirements.

Figure 7-1. Sample policy statement, National Science Foundation.

Here are some examples of these kinds of situations and the questions they might generate:

Scenario No. 1. Your project has been funded for a two-year period and includes money for the salary of a staff member who will be hired to conduct the bulk of project activities. The person you originally had in mind has taken another position, however, and two months pass while you advertise, interview candidates, and then wait for the successful applicant to serve out her notice at an existing job before joining your firm. What happens to the two months' unspent salary? Can you apply it to other project activities?

Scenario No. 2. Your proposal stated four specific objectives that you planned to accomplish. Early in the project, however, it becomes apparent that one of them is unattainable. Can you amend this one objective or, even better, delete it entirely?

Scenario No. 3. A new software program becomes available which would be useful in completing your project. The cost is $700. You would like to purchase it from grant funds, shifting the necessary funds from funds which were budgeted for travel. Will this be a problem?

Scenario No. 4. You had planned to buy a computer, and had budgeted it at $3500. But prices have dropped since the proposal was written, and you can get a comparable machine for $2000. Can you use the remaining $1500 to buy a fax machine?

Questions such as these may arise with any funded program. The key point to remember is that whenever such questions do come up, you must do two things:

1. Know the rules that apply to this particular agency and/or program.
2. Follow them within both the letter and the spirit of the rules.

"Knowing the rules" doesn't necessarily mean memorizing every applicable regulation but simply finding out what the rules are in each particular case. Often, this may be accomplished by consulting the written materials mentioned above.

If written guidelines are unavailable or unclear, contact your project officer or other appropriate official. Explain your question, and then take action according to the advice given. In the process, try to obtain written documentation of approval for any changes. This can be done by posing the question in writing and waiting for a written response or by sending a letter confirming a telephone conversation. In any case, it is always wise to document any approvals for deviation from initially approved plans.

Operating a Successful Project

In general, the same principles of good management which apply to any business situation will serve you well in administering a grant or contract project. In addition, keep in mind the following:

1. The U.S. government thrives on paperwork. Even if you do not agree with this philosophy, playing the game means completing reports and maintaining lots of documentation. Be sure to keep adequate records about your project.

2. Public funds bring extra responsibilities. When you receive funds from a public agency, always understand that you are subject to special government regulations. Be sure to follow the appropriate laws and policies at all times.

3. Successful projects can often lead to more funding. Many projects are extended or renewed beyond the initial funding period. Others help companies build a track record, which helps in obtaining new awards. If you do a good job, you may find yourself in a position to obtain additional grants or contracts.

8
Building Key Relationships

No business enterprise operates in a vacuum, and the same is true for special projects funded by government agencies. Despite the tendency of the government to operate as a faceless bureaucracy, dealing with the government means not just filling out written forms but also dealing directly with people. The more effectively you can interact with men and women in key positions, the better your chances of obtaining funds and completing successful projects.

Relationships at the Prefunding Stage

In attempting to obtain grant or contract funding, it can be helpful to make contact with officials who may be in a position:

1. To explain program regulations
2. To listen to an idea for a proposal and give an opinion as to whether it might be worth developing
3. To review a draft proposal and make suggestions for improvement
4. To provide information on other sources of funding
5. To alert you of upcoming changes or new programs which have not been officially announced
6. To provide names of other officials, departments, or agencies that might be helpful
7. To provide other types of assistance

The type of assistance which might be obtained varies widely from one program to the next and from individual to individual. This means you need to be flexible in dealing with government officials at the preproposal stage. Ideally, such flexibility involves being sensitive to the particular styles of operation of the officials with whom you communicate and then adjusting your tactics accordingly.

For example, say you see an announcement in a newsletter about a grant program for which small businesses are eligible. A contact, Roger White, is listed and a phone number in Washington, DC, is given. You call the number, but Mr. White is not in, and you ask that he return your call. After two days your call has not been returned, so you try again. This time, you reach Mr. White, who makes no mention of your earlier call. You begin asking a few simple questions, but his responses are curt and devoid of friendliness or enthusiasm. He seems anxious to conclude the conversation, so you keep the call short and hang up.

What should you conclude? It is possible that you simply caught Mr. White at a bad time. But what is more likely is that he wants to limit contact with potential applicants. Rather than irritating him, the best approach may be to "back off" and concentrate exclusively on the writing of the proposal itself.

Another time, you may respond to a similar announcement and have quite different results. This time the contact person, Diana Anderson, seems highly interested in your questions. You talk with her for nearly 15 minutes about the central idea for your proposal, and some questions you have about the program are clarified in the process. One answer in particular, about the agency's preferences for research projects over other kinds of activities, helps you decide between two courses of action you had been considering.

You can never know what to expect in dealing with government officials and staff members. Some of them are career bureaucrats who avoid doing more than provide the bare minimum of information. They may feel that the less said, the smaller the chance that anyone will pursue additional details, misunderstand anything they have said, or cause any need for time-consuming follow-up.

Some other contacts may be academic types who have taken leave from a college or university to work temporarily for a government agency. They may enjoy talking with potential applicants and try to be very accommodating. Still other officials may come from any number of backgrounds and have any of a wide variety of outlooks and work styles. They may be lazy or energetic, rude or polite, agency veterans or new employees who want to impress everyone with their helpfulness.

Where personalities are not an issue, policies or practices within agencies or program areas may dictate the kind of cooperation you might expect. One agency may encourage its personnel to work closely with applications, while another may prohibit or discourage such interaction. Even within agencies, one department or program may operate quite differently from another in this regard.

Given these variations, it may not always be possible to foster working relationships with government officials. But when the situation allows, this practice makes sense. First of all, you can obtain tremendously helpful information by communicating with people in the know. Having a knowledgeable staff member tell you that an idea holds promise, for example, can be a good indicator as you begin proposal development. On the other hand, the response may be that the idea seems to have flaws or doesn't fit the priorities of the program or is too similar to some other projects which have recently been funded. In that event, one conversation could save you a great deal of work that stands little chance of paying off.

At the same time, any contact with the right people can hold potential benefit. If an agency official expresses interest in a proposal, he or she may become an advocate for it at a later stage. Even if this is not the case, the fact that you have had telephone conversations or other contacts makes each of you a "real person" to the other, rather than just a name. This never hurts and in fact could prove helpful at some later date.

Relationships during the Award Period

Maintaining personal relationships can be even more important once your project has been funded. A good working relationship with officials at the sponsoring agency can help ensure a smoothly running project.

This may seem obvious, but surprisingly, for many programs, no such communication is required. Once you receive a written award notification, there may be little or no direct communication with the funding agency, except for occasional form letters about reports or other administrative matters. In some cases, a project can be successfully completed with very little direct communication between the project director and agency officials. In other instances, however, a lack of communication can lead to problems or misunderstandings. What if you make what you consider a minor change in the budget only to find at the end of the project that this was not allowable? Or what happens if you need help toward the end of the project but have had no previous contacts with agency officials? A much better approach is to open channels of communication and keep them open.

In developing good communications, the first step is knowing whom to contact. As noted earlier, award letters usually provide the name and phone number of at least one person who will be responsible as a contact person for your project. If such information is not made clear at the outset of your project, be aggressive and obtain it by calling or writing the person who sent the award letter. Then keep this information where it will be readily available.

In some cases, the names of more than one individual will be provided. You might have one person to contact regarding programmatic matters, for example, and another for budgetary details. In this eventuality, keep both names handy and contact whichever one seems most appropriate for each matter being addressed.

When you have questions, don't hesitate to call or write an agency contact person. This can have a double value: you obtain authoritative advice, and the official becomes accustomed to hearing from you and thus may be more responsive than would otherwise be the case if additional help is needed at a later date.

However, don't let the importance of keeping in touch with officials lead you to think more is necessarily better. Most government staffers *do not* want to hear from you unless there is a legitimate reason. Too many phone calls or letters may lead them to consider you a pest. Working with agency officials is not the same as cultivating a sales prospect or other business contact. Occasional, issue-oriented contacts are usually the best approach.

Other Points of Contact

In addition to representatives of agencies sponsoring projects in which you are interested, other contacts can prove helpful. Some examples are as follows:

Your congressional representative and his or her staff may be helpful in alerting you to new programs or funding opportunities.

It may be useful to contact the nearest Small Business Administration office or Office of Small and Disadvantaged Business Utilization (SADBU; see Chap. 9 for addresses). You might want to submit a capability statement to the latter, for example, which outlines interests and capabilities of your company. You might ask SADBU officials to refer you to other agencies, or you might ask that your name be placed on appropriate mailing lists.

If other companies in your area are active in proposal development, it could be useful to get to know one or more persons experienced in this area and then exchange information or proposal development tips. This can be especially fruitful if your companies deal in different products and thus won't be competing with one another. A local small business office or chamber of commerce might help identify such businesses or individuals. Others around the country can be identified by contacting agencies which fund small businesses and asking for a list of recent grantees.

Personnel who work for nonprofit agencies such as colleges, arts organizations, and city governments can become useful contacts. They may know of possibilities for public-private partnerships, for instance. Or you may want to consider hiring them to help write proposals or evaluate funded projects if they have had previous experience with grant or contract projects at the nonprofit level.

Because of efforts to make the process of awarding grants and contracts a fair one, the personal touch is not always advisable. You never want it to appear, for example, that you are asking for special consideration or any type of unfair advantage. At the same time, honing and using your "people skills" can help in obtaining some types of awards. After all, people respond to other people. And if you are diligent in building and maintaining appropriate contacts, the effort can often pay substantial dividends.

9 Winning Procurement Contracts

While the emphasis in this book is on grants and contracts to support special projects sponsored by the government, the other broad category of government contracts should not be overlooked. This is the area of procurement contracts.

Procurement contracts are agreements through which the government purchases goods or services (*procure* simply means to acquire or obtain something). This represents an enormous area of potential, not just for larger businesses but also for smaller firms. After all, the United States government is one of the largest consumers of goods and services in the entire world.

Billions of dollars are expended every hear to keep government agencies in operation. Whether keeping an aircraft carrier and its crew of 4000 sailors supplied with everything from weapons to toilet paper, or providing consulting assistance for the Department of Energy (to cite just two examples), businesses of all types find the federal government a highly desirable customer.

Special Preferences for Small Businesses

Small businesses are not only eligible to compete for procurement contracts but they actually receive preference over larger firms in some cases, thanks to several laws and government policies designed to help small businesses obtain a fair share of government contracts. Examples include:

- *Small Business Set-Asides.* Some competitions for government business are limited exclusively to small businesses. Under the provisions of the Small Business Act, federal agencies set up such programs so that smaller firms will not always be faced with the task of competing against much larger companies. If you apply for a contract of this type, it will still be necessary to offer competitive pricing, but your competitors will all be small businesses—making the odds of success higher than might otherwise be the case.

- *Office of Small and Disadvantaged Business Utilization.* Since 1978, each major government agency has been required by law to operate an Office of Small and Disadvantaged Business Utilization. This office promotes participation by firms which might otherwise be left out of the procurement process.

For information about the office's services, you may write or telephone as follows:

Office of Small and Disadvantaged Business Utilization
18th and F Streets NW
Washington, DC 20405
(202) 566-1021

The addresses of each agency's office are listed in Table 9-1.

Table 9-1. Offices of Small and Disadvantaged Business Utilization

Agency for International Development Director, OSDBU, Room 648 SA14 Rosslyn, VA 22209 (703) 235-1720	Department of the Air Force Director, OSDBU, Room 4C255 Washington, DC 20330-5040 (202) 697-4126
Defense Logistics Agency Director, OSDBU, Room 4B110 Alexandria, VA 22304-6100 (703) 274-6471	Department of the Army Director, OSDBU, Room 2A712 Washington, DC 20310 (202) 695-9800
Department of Agriculture Director, OSDBU, Room 127W Washington, DC 20503 (202) 395-3314	Department of Commerce Director, OSDBU, Room 6411 Washington, DC 20230 (202) 377-3387

(*Continued*)

Table 9-1. Offices of Small and Disadvantaged Business Utilization (*Continued*)

Department of Defense
Director, OSDBU, Room 2A340
Washington, DC 20301
(202) 694-1151

Department of Education
Director, OSDBU, Room 2141
Washington, DC 20202
(202) 245-9582

Department of Energy
Director, OSDBU, Room 1E061
Washington, DC 20585
(202) 252-8201

Department of Health and Human Services
Director, OSDBU, Room 513D
Washington, DC 20201
(202) 245-7300

Department of Housing and Urban Development
Director, OSDBU, Room 10226
Washington, DC 20410
(202) 755-1428

Department of the Interior
Director, OSDBU, Room 2747
Washington, DC 20240
(202) 343-8493

Department of Justice
Director, OSDBU
Room 748, HOLC Building
Washington, DC 20530
(202) 724-6271

Department of Labor
Director, OSDBU, Room S1004
Washington, DC 20210
(202) 523-9148

Department of the Navy
Director, OSDBU, Room 604
Crystal Plaza, Building 6
Washington, DC 20360
(202) 692-7122

Department of State
Director, OSDBU, Room 513 (SA-6)
Washington, DC 20520
(202) 235-9579

Department of Transportation
Director, OSDBU, Room 10222
Washington, DC 20250
(202) 426-1930

Department of the Treasury
Director, OSDBU, Room 127W
Washington, DC 20250
(202) 447-7117

Department of Veterans Affairs
Director, OSDBU
810 Vermont Avenue, NW, Room 005C
Washington, DC 20420
(202) 376-6996

Environmental Protection Agency
Director, OSDBU, Room 1108
CM No 2 Code Al49C
Washington, DC 29460
(202) 557-7777

Executive Office of the President
Director, OSDBU
Washington, DC 20503
(202) 395-3314

Export-Import Bank of the United States
Director, OSDBU, Room 1031
Washington, DC 20571
(202) 566-8111

Federal Home Loan Bank Board
Director, OSDBU, Room G-3, 4th Floor
Washington, DC 20552
(202) 377-6245

Federal Trade Commission
Director, OSDBU, Room 850
Washington, DC 20580
(202) 523-5552

General Services Administration
Director, OSDBU, Room 6017
Washington, DC 20405
(202) 566-1021

National Aeronautics and Space Administration
Director, OSDBU
Headquarters, Code K
Washington, DC 20504
(202) 453-2088

Table 9-1. Offices of Small and Disadvantaged Business Utilization (*Continued*)

National Credit Union Administration
Director, OSDBU
1776 G Street NW, Room 6630
Washington, DC 20456
(202) 357-1025

National Science Foundation
Director, OSDBU
1800 G Street NW, Room 511A
Washington, DC 20550
(202) 357-5000

Nuclear Regulatory Commission
Director, OSDBU
Maryland National Bank Building
Room 7217
Washington, DC 20555
(202) 492-4665

Railroad Retirement Board
Director, OSDBU
844 North Rush Street, Room 1230
Chicago, IL 60611
(312) 751-4565

Tennessee Valley Authority
Director, OSDBU
1000 Commerce Union Bank Building
Chattanooga, TN 37401
(615) 751-2624

U.S. Information Agency
Director, OSDBU
400 6th Street SW, Room 1719
Washington, DC 20457
(202) 619–4700

U.S. Postal Service
Director, OSDBU
475 L'Enfant Plaza West SW, Room 1340
Washington, DC 20260-6201
(202) 268-4633

- *Socially and Economically Disadvantaged Businesses.* A provision of the Small Business Act allows the Small Business Administration (SBA) to contract with other government agencies to provide goods or services and then subcontract with qualified small businesses for these goods or services.

  For those companies which are certified by the Small Business Administration as eligible, contracts may be awarded on a noncompetitive basis. This can be a real boon for struggling companies or those finding it difficult to compete for procurement contracts.

  To qualify, a company must:

1. Be a small business
2. Be at least 51 percent owned by one or more "socially and economically disadvantaged" individuals, which include the following as defined in SBA legislation:
   - Blacks
   - Hispanics
   - Native Americans
   - Asian or Pacific Americans

3. Be certified as eligible by the Small Business Administration

- *Subcontracting Requirements.* Another government practice that is helpful for small businesses involves large contracts awarded to corporations or other larger businesses. Here, firms landing large contracts (over $500,000 or, in the case of construction projects, over $1 million) are required to set goals for awarding subcontracts to small businesses. This opens the doors for a number of small businesses.

Pursuing Procurement Contracts

Programs giving preference to small businesses can be particularly helpful, but they do not represent the only opportunities for small firms. The government takes pains to ensure that its procurement practices are fair and open to everyone. Of course abuses sometimes occur (often making headlines), but the truth is that any company, large or small, has a fair chance to do business with the federal government. Following is an overview of how these contracts are handled.

Types of Government Purchases

Government agencies make two basic kinds of purchases:

1. Items or services for general use (such as office furniture, computers, consultant services in personnel management, automobiles, paper goods, fax machines, paper clips, building construction, custodial services, and so forth)
2. Specialized equipment, services, or supplies (such as radiation-monitoring equipment for the Department of Energy, combat fatigues for the army or Marine Corps, mass transit feasibility studies for the Department of Transportation, and so on)

Depending on the type of business you operate, either or both types of purchases might represent possibilities worth pursuing for your firm.

General-use items are usually purchased through the General Services Administration (GSA), the Defense Logistics Agency (DLA), and the Veterans Administration (VA). The General Services Administration obtains supplies, services, and equipment for many government agencies, spending billions of dollars every year. The largest single consumer among government agencies is the Department of Defense (DOD), which obtains general-use items such as office furniture and cleaning supplies through the GSA.

Specialized items are often obtained directly by the agency seeking them rather than by the General Services Administration. For example, the Department of the Army operates the Army Materiel Command, which purchases materiel needed for army units around the world. It is headquartered in Arlington, Virginia. Other agencies operate in a similar fashion. So keep in mind that while the GSA spends more dollars every year than do most countries, it is by no means the only game in town. Individual agencies also have their own particular needs which in many cases can be met by small businesses.

Just how do you pursue procurement contracts? The first step is finding out what needs might be met by your business. This can be accomplished in any of the following ways:

1. Review announcements published in *Commerce Business Daily*, and then write or call for additional information as noted in the announcement (as discussed in Chap. 2; *Commerce Business Daily* is available from the U.S. Government Printing Office, Washington, DC 20402, as well as in libraries and some government offices).

2. Watch for advertisements in other publications or announcements posted in public places.

3. Have your firm's name placed on government mailing lists to receive solicitations by mail. You can have this done simply by providing the relevant details to any agency to which you are interested in submitting bids; after that you will begin receiving solicitation information on a routine basis.

The General Services Administration uses a decentralized approach in providing procurement information. To have your firm added to mailing lists maintained by this agency, contact one of the following GSA Service Centers:

For businesses in Washington, DC, and nearby Maryland and Virginia:	7th and D Streets SW, Room 1050 Washington, DC 20407 (202) 472-1804
For businesses in Connecticut, Maine, Massachusetts, New Hampshire, Rhode Island, and Vermont:	Tip O'Neill Federal Building 10 Causeway Street Boston, MA 02222 (617) 565-8100
For businesses in New Jersey, New York, Puerto Rico, and U.S. Virgin Islands:	26 Federal Plaza New York, NY 10278 (212) 264-1234
For businesses in Delaware, Pennsylvania, Maryland, Virginia, and West Virginia:	9th and Market Streets, Room 5151 Philadelphia, PA 19107 (215) 597-9613

For businesses in Alabama, Florida, Georgia, Kentucky, Mississippi, North Carolina, South Carolina, and Tennessee:	Richard B. Russell Federal Building 75 Spring Street Atlanta, GA 30303 (404) 331-5103
For businesses in Illinois, Indiana, Michigan, Minnesota, Ohio, and Wisconsin:	230 South Dearborn Street Chicago, IL 60604 (312) 353-5383
For businesses in Iowa, Kansas, Missouri, and Nebraska:	1500 East Bannister Road Kansas City, MO 64131 (816) 926-7203
For businesses in Arkansas, Louisiana, New Mexico, Oklahoma, and Texas:	819 Taylor Street Fort Worth, TX 76102 (817) 334-3284
For businesses in Colorado, Montana, North Dakota, South Dakota, Utah, and Wyoming:	Denver Federal Center, Building 41 Denver, CO 80225 (303) 236-7408
For businesses in Hawaii, Nevada (except for Clark County), and northern California:	525 Market Street San Francisco, CA 94105 (415) 974-0523
For businesses in Arizona, Los Angeles, Nevada (Clark County only), and southern California:	300 North Los Angeles Street Los Angeles, CA 90012 (213) 894-3210
For businesses in Alaska, Idaho, Oregon, and Washington:	15th and C Streets, SW Auburn, WA 98001 (206) 931-7956

Winning Contracts

Once you learn about opportunities for procurement contracts, the next step is submitting bids. Government agencies award bids on a competitive basis. The selection criteria are as follows:

- All "responsible offerors" may compete on an equal basis. Responsible offerors are those considered to have sufficient quality and stability to provide the service or product needed. This may include evaluation or consideration of such factors as:

  The company's production capabilities
  The firm's financial status, possibly including credit rating
  Quality-control factors
  Plant and testing facilities
  Performance with previous government contracts
  Overall integrity

Small businesses have a special kind of protection in this area thanks to the SBA. If a small business has a bid rejected because of lack of responsibility, the contracting officer is required to notify the SBA. If the SBA investigates and finds the company is competent to undertake the contract, it will issue a certificate of competency which the contracting officer must consider as binding for the competition on which this particular offer was based.

- All bids under any contract competition must be submitted by a specified date and time. Those which fail to meet the deadline will be disqualified.
- In many cases, bids must be sealed and will not be opened until after the deadline has passed and all proposals have been accepted.
- Each bid is reviewed, and the contract is awarded to the responsible offeror who submits the lowest price or to the bid that is judged most advantageous to the government for some other justifiable reason.

Getting Started

If you feel your company offers products or services which the government needs, why not pursue the possibility of bidding for procurement contracts?

To get started, contact the nearest Office of Small and Disadvantaged Business Utilization (see Table 9-1), and ask for assistance (be sure to mention that yours is a small business). Or, as mentioned previously, contact the closest GSA Service Center (addresses provided earlier in this chapter), and indicate your interest in bidding on supply and service requirements procured by the GSA. In response, you will receive the following:

Standard Form 129, Solicitation Mailing List Application

GSA Form 3038, Bidder's Mailing List Application Code Sheet

GSA Form 1382, List of Commodities and Services

GSA regional bidder's mailing list application, as appropriate

Review the materials and complete the forms provided, and you can be on your way to possible government business. Be sure also to check sources such as *Commerce Business Daily* for announcements about procurements, leads about possible subcontracts, and other information.

Also, make sure your firm is listed in the Procurement Automated Source System (PASS), an on-line list of small businesses and their capabilities. This is a free service available to any small business. Contact the nearest office of the Small Business Administration to request an application for a PASS listing (see list of SBA offices in your state in the appendix, or look under "U.S. Government" in your telephone directory).

Helpful Publications, Forms, and Other Materials

The government provides other resources for those interested in doing business with government agencies. Many are provided directly by the agency involved. Following is an overview of some of these informational items and where they may be obtained.

Your Business and the SBA is a pamphlet describing services provided by the Small Business Administration. It is available free at SBA field offices or by writing or calling the SBA at 1411 L Street NW, Washington, DC 20416.

Doing Business with the Federal Government, a source of material for this chapter, is an excellent overview of government business possibilities for large and small firms. It is available for $2.50 from the U.S. Government Printing Office, Washington, DC 20402.

If you are interested in selling to the military, a good place to start is with a copy of the publication, *Selling to the Military,* also available from the U.S. Government Printing Office. This publication provides an overview of military procurement practices and how businesses might pursue them.

A similar but more specialized publication is *Selling to the United States Air Force,* free from the Office of Small and Disadvantaged Business Utilization, HQ USAF/RDB, Washington, DC 20330-5040.

The *Guide to Defense Acquisition Regulation,* published by the Department of Defense, is available from the U.S. Government Printing Office at the address noted previously. It contains regulatory information of special interest to small businesses. The same office provides a directory, "Small and Disadvantaged Business Utilization Specialists," which lists small business specialists employed by the Defense Logistic Agency and various military departments. These individuals are available to provide small businesses with information on how to do business with military departments.

The following booklets about the Defense Logistics Agency (DLA) are available free from the Small and Disadvantaged Business Utilization Office, DLA, Cameron Station, 5010 Duke Street, Alexandria, VA 22314:

An Identification of Commodities Purchased by the DLA

An Introduction to the DLA

How to Do Business with the DLA

A listing of DLA supply centers appears as Table 9-2.

If you are interested in becoming a supplier to the DLA, contact the Small and Disadvantaged Business specialist at any of the centers listed in Table 9-2 which seem a good possibility for your business's products or services. Request Standard Form 129, the application form to be placed on appropriate mailing lists, and then complete and return it.

If your interest is in subcontracting, the appropriate point of contact is the Defense Contract Administration Services (DCAS). The best approach is to contact the Small and Disadvantaged Business specialist at one of the regional DCAS offices listed in Table 9-3.

Information about various civilian procurement programs is also available. For example, the pamphlet *Selling to the United States Department of Agriculture* not only includes an overview of purchasing practices of this large federal department but also lists agency purchasing offices along with their addresses. This free publication may be obtained by writing the U.S. Department of Agriculture, Office of Operations and Finance, Room 1575, South Building, Washington, DC 20250.

The U.S. Department of Energy provides a similar publication. *Doing Business with the Department of Energy* may be obtained free from the Department of Energy, Technical Information Center, P.O. Box 62, Oak Ridge, TN 37830. The *Guide for the Submission of Unsolicited Proposals* is available on request at the same address.

Table 9-2. Defense Logistics Agency Supply Centers

Defense Construction Supply Center 3990 East Broad Street Columbus, OH 43215 (614) 238-3541	Defense General Supply Center Bellwood, Petersburg Pike Richmond, VA 23297 (804) 275-3617 or 275-3287
Defense Electronics Supply Center 1507 Wilmington Pike Dayton, OH 45444 (513) 296-5231	Defense Industrial Supply Center 700 Robbins Avenue Philadelphia, PA 19111 (215) 697-2747
Defense Fuel Supply Center Cameron Station, Building 8 5010 Duke Street Alexandria, VA 22314 (202) 274-7428	Defense Personnel Support Center 2800 South 20th Street Philadelphia, PA 19101 (215) 952-2321

Table 9-3. Regional Office Locations of the Defense Contract Administration Services

805 Walker Street Marietta, GA 30060 (404) 429-6195	615 East Houston Street San Antonio, TX 78294 (512) 229-4650
495 Summer Street Boston, MA 02210 (617) 451-4317	215 North 7th Street Phoenix, AZ 85034 (602) 261-6177
O'Hare International Airport P.O. Box 66475 Chicago, IL 60666 (312) 694-6020	11099 South La Cienega Boulevard Los Angeles, CA 90045 (213) 643-0620
Federal Office Building 1240 East Ninth Street Cleveland, OH 44199 (216) 522-5122	201 Varick Street New York, NY 10014-4811 (212) 807-3050
1200 Main Tower Dallas, TX 75202 (214) 670-9205	

The huge Department of Health and Human Services, which includes agencies such as the Public Health Service and the Social Security Administration, will provide details about contracts and procurement needs on request. Write the Division of Contract and Grant Operations, Office of the Secretary, 200 Independence Avenue SW, Room 443H, Washington, DC 20201.

The Department of Housing and Urban Development procures many products related to housing and property management. For information, contact the Office of Procurement and Contracts, Administration Support Division, U.S. Department of Housing and Urban Development, 451 Seventh Street SW, Washington, DC 20410.

The following bulletins may be obtained from the Department of Veterans Affairs:

Could You Use a Multibillion Dollar Customer?

Doing Business with the Department of Veterans Affairs

Let's Do Business

Request them from the Office of Procurement and Supply, Department of Veterans Affairs, 810 Vermont Avenue NW, Washington, DC 20420.

The Postal Service's similar brochure is *Let's Do Business,* available from the Office of Contracts, Documents Processing Branch, Procurement and Supply Department, U.S. Postal Service, 475 L'Enfant Plaza SW, Washington, DC 20260-6232.

For any other agencies, contact the appropriate Office of Small and Disadvantaged Business Utilization as listed in Table 9-1.

10 Playing the Game

Now that you have an overview of the grant and contract process, you should be ready to pursue funding possibilities for your company. Don't let the technical aspects of this work put you off—almost anyone can master the basics of proposal development with some practice.

Look at it as a game. Playing chess or bridge, for example, may look quite complicated to the uninitiated, but with a little time or effort most people can learn the basics. The same is true of the grant and contract game. And with the latter, the potential payoff for your firm can be substantial.

Five Keys to Success

For any small business, success in grant and contract development rests on several basic factors. Here are five keys to succeeding in this competitive but promising arena.

1. *Be aggressive.* Except in rare instances, grant and contract awards will never be forthcoming unless you make them happen. Landing an award is nothing like winning the state lottery, where everything rests on chance. This is an area where hard work can pay off handsomely. If you are willing to aggressively pursue funding possibilities, the chance for success always awaits you.

2. *Be creative.* Since grant and contract applications require the same basic information from everyone who applies, one application tends to look much like the next. If you can come up with a creative

angle for solving a problem or addressing a funding priority, you have a better chance of getting funded. Use your imagination to help make your proposals stand out from the competition.

3. *Be thorough.* One of the most common weaknesses in grant and contract proposals is the submission of material which is only partially explained. Even worse, required information is sometimes left out entirely. Make certain your proposals are thorough and complete. Review them carefully before final submission, and compare the finished product with the application guidelines.

4. *Be persistent.* If you submit proposals, some will be turned down. In fact, you may face any number of failures, but don't let this deter you. Many successful grantees have found that persistence pays off. This is a highly competitive process, and a negative response does not mean you should give up on any one idea or program. Instead, keep trying until your work pays off.

5. *Keep close tabs on application efforts.* If you are submitting multiple proposals, be sure to keep track of your efforts so that you won't forget the status of each one. A good idea is to develop a tracking system to help you follow the progress of proposals. This can be especially useful if you submit the same basic idea to multiple sources or develop several different proposals. Figure 10-1 is a simple report which can be developed for this purpose.

Learn from Others

Any time you develop a proposal, the work can provide a learning experience. The more practice you gain, the better your proposals should become.

To help in this process, be sure to obtain reviewers' comments about proposals you have submitted. Federal agencies are required by law to provide this information if you request it. What you will usually get is a photocopy of rating sheets completed by the people who reviewed your application, often including written comments and criticisms. Having this information can help you improve areas of weakness and develop stronger proposals in the future.

Reviewers' comments are not available until after the review process has been completed for all applications, and even then it may take several weeks to receive them. But don't let this delay keep you from using this as a learning opportunity. After all, all you need to do is send a simple letter. A sample is provided as Fig. 10-2.

Topic	Funding source	Date submitted	Amount requested	Status

INSTRUCTIONS: If you submit multiple grant or contract proposals, use this form to keep track of them. Several submissions can be listed on each copy of the form, either in chronological or alphabetical order. If necessary, under "Topic," fill in a shortened version of the proposal title rather than the full descriptive title. Abbreviations or acronyms such as NASA or NSF work best under "Funding source." Under "Status," make a notation such as "under consideration," "funded," or "not funded." It is important to keep information on status updated so that future action can be based on accurate details. For example, if no response has been received six months after the date listed under "Date submitted," a follow-up inquiry may be in order.

Figure 10-1. Sample submission tracking form.

A Proposal Development Task List

Use the list in Fig. 10-3 as a worksheet for planning and developing grant or contract proposals. Note that not every item will be pertinent for every proposal (for example, if an abstract is not required, you might choose to skip it). In using this form, you might want to:

1. Make photocopies and use them to write on as you work through proposals

Your Letterhead Here

(Agency Address)

To Whom It May Concern:

My organization recently submitted a proposal under the ____________________________ program. The application number assigned to the project was ______________.

Please send me reviewers' comments for this proposal, plus any other related information you might care to share.

Thank you for consideration of this request.

Sincerely,

(Name of project director)

Figure 10-2. Sample request for reviewers' comments.

2. Have the list duplicated via word processor or computer
3. Share copies with colleagues as work progresses items are checked off to keep them informed of progress, or simply use the task list for your own follow-up purposes.

For each item listed, place an X or a check mark in the space provided when that item has been completed. Mark those that are not applicable *NA,* or just leave inapplicable items blank.

Have Fun

Certainly, proposal development requires hard work, but it can be enjoyable too. The satisfaction of putting together a strong application, combined with the air of competition involved in the process, can make this a challenging activity.

So have some fun! Take a look at the possibilities that await your small business in the grant and contract area. Then if you feel some potential exists, go for it! Here's hoping that you can join the thousands of other small companies that have benefited from government funding.

____
Name of program and/or funding source

____
Date due

1. Preproposal Stage

_____ Funding source identified

_____ Guidelines requested

  _____ Phone call

  _____ Letter

  _____ Other: ____________________________

  _____ Date requested

_____ Guidelines received

  _____ Date received

_____ Guidelines read or reviewed

_____ Guidelines shared with others:

  ______________________________ Name

  ______________________________ Name

  ______________________________ Name

_____ Eligibility determined

_____ Chances for success assessed (i.e., is there enough chance of receiving funding to justify the work of proposal preparation?)

_____ Commitment made to apply

_____ Internal deadlines established

_____ Extra copies of proposal forms photocopied

Figure 10-3. Proposal development task list.

2. Background and/or Planning Stage

_____ Literature review conducted

_____ Background reading done

_____ Supportive statistics requested and gathered

_____ Questions clarified and/or additional information requested

_____ Basic idea(s) for proposal formulated

_____ For basic idea(s), key questions considered:

 _____ What would be done?

 _____ Who would do it?

 _____ Why would the funding source be interested (i.e., how is the idea different from or better than other approaches)?

 _____ Do I (or others in my firm) have the necessary background and/or competencies to carry out the project if funded?

 _____ Is there a genuine need for the project?

3. Preliminary Writing Stage

_____ Rough outline of proposal developed

_____ Major headings listed for addressing each section and/or selection criterion

_____ Introduced and/or background statement developed in rough form

_____ Need or problem statement developed in rough form

_____ First draft of goal statement(s) written

_____ First draft of specific objectives written

_____ First draft of project narrative written, including some or all of these:

 _____ Activities planned

 _____ Rationale for plan of action and/or activities

Figure 10-3 *(Continued)*

____ Timetable for implementation of activities

____ Supporting details for plan of action

____ Key personnel

4. Preliminary Budget Stage

____ Upper and lower limits of funding possibilities determined

____ Target range and amount for proposed budget identified

____ Salaries calculated for any proposed positions

____ Fringe benefits calculated

____ Estimates of equipment costs obtained from vendors

____ Travel costs estimated (if necessary, information obtained from airlines or travel agency)

____ Costs of supplies estimated

____ Other costs identified or estimated

____ Total direct costs calculated

____ Total indirect costs calculated

5. Proposal Expansion and/or Enhancement Phase

____ Rough draft shared with others

____ Abstract written

____ Table of contents developed

____ Tables and/or graphs added

____ Narrative expanded and/or improved

____ Goals reviewed and/or revised

____ Objectives reviewed and/or revised

____ Timetable finalized

____ Expected outcomes listed

____ Basic ideas developed and/or explained

____ Evaluation strategies developed and/or explained

____ Appendixes added

____ Résumés of key personnel added

Figure 10-3 *(Continued)*

6. Editing and Completion Stage

_____ Contents checked against application instructions to make certain each selection criterion is addressed

_____ Manuscript checked for spelling and grammar

_____ Assurances completed and signed

_____ Cover sheet completed

_____ Budget forms typed

_____ Budget figures checked

_____ Page numbers added

_____ Text enhanced (with spacing, underlining, etc.)

_____ Entire proposal reviewed for clarity and thoroughness

7. Submission Stage

_____ Checklist reviewed (if provided in application package)

_____ Copies prepared per application instructions

_____ Acknowledgement card prepared

_____ Original signatures provided on one completed copy

_____ Completed proposal stapled, placed in notebooks, or otherwise organized and/or bound according to application instructions

_____ Certified mail paperwork, commercial carrier paperwork, or other proof of transmittal prepared and copy retained

_____ Proposal mailed or transmitted in accordance with instructions

8. Follow-up Stage

_____ Acknowledgment card received

_____ Acknowledgment card stapled to file copy of proposal

_____ Application number noted on acknowledgment card and retained for possible future correspondence

_____ Copy of proposal kept near phone in case of phone responses

_____ Copies of any follow-up correspondence retained

_____ Reviewers' comments obtained after notification of acceptance or nonacceptance

Figure 10-3 *(Continued)*

Appendix A
Glossary of Selected Terms

abstract: A concise overview of a proposed project or one that has been funded.

assurances: Forms indicating that the applicant ensures it will meet certain regulations associated with federal programs.

award letter: Notification in writing that a grant or contract has been awarded; usually includes amount and duration of award.

consultant: An individual retained to conduct specific activities such as training, evaluation, or other functions but not as a continuing or regular employee.

continuation award: An award continuing a grant beyond its initial funding period; if designated as "noncompeting," renewal will not be based on competition with other applicants.

contract: An agreement between a funding agency and an individual or organization under which the latter agrees to provide goods, services, or other specified products.

deadline: The date by which an application must be (1) received by the funding agency or (2) transmitted by the applicant to receive consideration for possible funding.

demonstration project: A project designed to try out an idea or methodology for possible future application or implementation.

direct costs: Expenses for a grant or contract project which can be specifically accounted for within standard budget categories such as personnel or equipment.

dissemination: The distribution or sharing of products, results of a project, or information resulting from the project.

evaluation: A formal assessment of the effectiveness of a project or any of the activities, goals, objectives, or other components which make up the project.

fiscal year: The budget year, which for the federal government is October 1 through September 30 but may last from July 1 through June 30 for state governments or federally funded state-level programs.

fixed-unit price: The price per unit necessary to attain the goals specified in the contract.

formative evaluation: Assessment of a process, activity, or other effort while the effort is still underway.

grant: An award made to an individual or organization; it may or may not come with preconditions but in either case need not be repaid.

grantback: The return to a grant recipient of a portion of the funds recovered by the funding agency as a result of an audit or other finding.

grantee: The recipient of a grant.

grantor: The agency or other organization which awards a grant.

in-kind contribution: A portion of a project contributed by the applicant; usually refers to existing resources rather than actual monetary expenditures.

intended outcomes: Changes or results expected as a result of a project or any of its component activities.

invitational priority: A special priority identified in a request for proposals (RFP) or other notification of proposed funding; applicants may be encouraged to develop proposals which address a priority area within a given competition.

negotiation: Review or discussion of proposed changes, often referring to changes made in a proposed budget before it becomes official.

peer review: The process of having proposals reviewed by persons working in the field being addressed or otherwise having appropriate qualifications; normally these reviewers are retained by the funding agency for the specific purpose of reviewing proposals under a single competition.

performance-based contract: A contract, usually fixed-price in nature, in which payment is made in accordance with the degree to which goals have been successfully attained.

principal investigator: The individual responsible for seeing that project activities are carried out as proposed; this term is usually used in research projects.

project director: The individual with legal responsibility for expending project funds and overseeing project activities; sometimes used interchangeably with *principal investigator.*

RFP: A request for proposals for a grant, contract, or other competition.

selection criteria: Preestablished points against which proposals are judged, often accompanied by a point scale for calculated of proposal scores during the review and selection process.

solicited proposal: A proposal which has been requested through a request for proposals or other notification that proposals are invited.

summative evaluation: Evaluation conducted after the activity being assessed has taken place.

title: A section of a bill considered or enacted by Congress; may be used to designate programs offered as a result of this legislation.

unsolicited proposal: A proposal which is submitted without having been requested.

vita: A résumé.

Appendix B Selected Abbreviations for Government Agencies, Programs, and Services

AID: Agency for International Development

BSC: Business Service Center

CFR: *Code of Federal Regulations*

DLA: Defense Logistics Agency

DOA: Department of Agriculture

DOD: Department of Defense

DOE: Department of Education

DOJ: Department of Justice

DOT: Department of Transportation

EPA: Environmental Protection Agency

FAR: Federal Acquisition Regulation

FIRMR: Federal Information Resources Management Regulations

FPMR: Federal Property Management Regulations

GAO: General Accounting Office

GSA: General Services Administration

HHS: Department of Health and Human Services

NASA: National Aeronautics and Space Administration

NRC: Nuclear Regulatory Commission

NSF: National Science Foundation

OSDBU: Office of Small and Disadvantaged Business Utilization

PASS: Procurement Automated Source System

SBA: Small Business Administration

SBIR: Small Business Innovation Research Program

TVA: Tennessee Valley Authority

VA: Veterans Administration

Appendix C
Locations and Telephone Numbers of Small Business Administration Information Offices

Alabama

Birmingham (205) 254-1755
Huntsville (205) 295-5326
Mobile (205) 690-2371
Montgomery (205) 832-7310

Alaska

Anchorage (907) 271-3650

Arizona

Phoenix (602) 261-3294

Tucson (602) 792-6301

California

Fresno (209) 487-5069

Sacramento (916) 440-3171

San Diego (714) 293-6640

Colorado

Colorado Springs (303) 635-8911

Denver (303) 236-7613

Connecticut

Hartford (203) 244-3540

New Haven (203) 773-2345

Florida

Jacksonville (904) 791-2791

Tampa (813) 228-2351

Georgia

Savannah (912) 944-4208

Thomasville (912) 226-2716

Hawaii

Honolulu (808) 546-7516

Idaho

Boise (208) 384-1242

Illinois

Springfield (217) 525-4270

Indiana

Indianapolis (317) 269-6234

Iowa

Des Moines (515) 284-4114

Kentucky

Covington (513) 684-1393
Louisville (502) 582-6436

Louisiana

Shreveport (318) 226-5006

Maine

Augusta (207) 622-6171

Maryland

Baltimore (301) 922-7611

Massachusetts

Andover (617) 681-5504
Worcester (617) 793-0408

Michigan

Detroit (313) 226-4910

Minnesota

St. Paul (Ft. Snelling) (612) 725-4015

Mississippi

Jackson (601) 960-4449

Tupelo (601) 842-0613

Montana

Billings (406) 657-6279

Helena (406) 449-5285

Missoula (406) 329-3117

Nevada

Las Vegas (702) 385-6444

Reno (702) 784-5302

New Hampshire

Manchester (603) 666-7581

New Jersey

Newark (201) 645-2416

Trenton (609) 989-2082

New Mexico

Albuquerque (505) 766-2101

Santa Fe (505) 988-6361

New York

Albany (518) 472-5447

Brooklyn (New York City) (718) 330-7474

Buffalo (716) 846-4588

Plattsburg (518) 563-0860

Rochester (716) 263-6288

Syracuse (315) 423-5424

North Carolina

Asheville (704) 258-2850

Raleigh (919) 755-4680

North Dakota

Bismarck (701) 255-4011

Fargo (701) 237-5771

Ohio

Cincinnati (513) 684-2306

Cleveland (216) 522-4220

Columbus (614) 469-6824

Oklahoma

Muskogee (918) 687-2283

Oklahoma City (405) 231-4791

Tulsa (918) 581-7755

Oregon

Eugene (503) 687-6640

Pennsylvania

Erie (814) 452-2903

Puerto Rico

Hato Rey (809) 753-4370

Rhode Island

Providence (401) 528-4492

South Carolina

Charleston (803) 724-4233

Columbia (803) 765-5581

South Dakota

Aberdeen (605) 225-0250

Pierre (605) 224-5852

Tennessee

Memphis (901) 521-3675

Nashville (615) 251-5221

Oak Ridge (615) 576-0583

Texas

Austin (512) 482-5751

Beaumont (713) 839-2501

Dallas (214) 767-0084

El Paso (915) 534-6262

Houston (713) 229-2732

Laredo (512) 723-6642

Lubbock (806) 762-7401

San Antonio (512) 229-6040

Utah

Odgen (801) 625-6764

Salt Lake City (801) 524-5260

Vermont

Burlington (802) 951-6364

Virginia

Richmond (804) 771-2101

Roanoke (703) 442-8551

West Virginia

Parkersburg (304) 420-6034

Wisconsin

Milwaukee (414) 291-3035

Wyoming

Casper/Mills (307) 221-5427

Cheyenne (307) 778-2220

Appendix D

Sample RFP

Following is a sample request for proposals (RFP) issued by a government agency (in this case, the National Aeronautics and Space Administration). For this competition, small businesses are the only eligible applicants.

Please note that the length and type of information contained in RFPs may vary widely. Contract RFPs tend to differ from those for grants in that they contain more details about obligations of the successful applicant and other related information.

In either case, the RFP can serve as a set of directions for preparing a proposal. If you read the instructions carefully and provide all information requested, you can complete a competitive proposal even if this is your first attempt at such a project.

NATIONAL AERONAUTICS AND SPACE ADMINISTRATION 1990 PROGRAM SOLICITATION SMALL BUSINESS INNOVATION RESEARCH

1.0 PROGRAM DESCRIPTION

1.1 Summary

The National Aeronautics and Space Administration (NASA) invites small business firms to submit Phase I proposals under its Small Business Innovation Research (SBIR) Program Solicitation 90-1. Firms with research or research and development capabilities in science or engineering in any of the areas listed are encouraged to participate.

This, the eighth annual SBIR solicitation by NASA, describes the program, identifies eligibility requirements, outlines the required proposal format and content, states proposal preparation and submission requirements, describes the proposal evaluation and award selection process, and provides other information to assist those interested in participating in NASA's SBIR program. It also identifies, in Section 8.0 and Appendix E, the technical topics and subtopics in which SBIR Phase I proposals are solicited in 1990. These topics and subtopics cover a broad range of current NASA interests, but do not necessarily include all areas in which NASA plans or currently conducts research. High-risk, high pay-off innovations are desired.

For planning purposes, NASA expects to select approximately 275 high quality research or research and development (R/R&D) proposals for Phase I contract awards based on this Solicitation. Phase I contracts are for six months duration and may be funded up to $50,000, including profit. Selections will be based on the competitive merits of the offering and on NASA needs and priorities.

For planning purposes, NASA anticipates that approximately 50 percent of the Phase I projects – those deemed to have the highest feasibility and greatest value to NASA – will be selected competitively for further development under Phase II continuations. The Phase II period of performance and funding will depend on the project scope, but will normally not exceed 24 months and $500,000. Phase II competition is limited to Phase I contractors.

1.2 Program Features

Legislative Basis. The Small Business Innovation Development Act of 1982, 15 U.S.C. 638, P.L. 97-219 was enacted July 22, 1982 and was reauthorized by P.L. 99-443 on October 6, 1986. SBIR Program Guidelines are provided by the Small Business Administration Policy Directive for SBIR whose current revision became effective on June 28, 1988.

Objectives. SBIR program objectives include stimulating technological innovation in the private sector, strengthening the role of small business in meeting Federal research and development needs, increasing the commercial application of Federally supported research results, and fostering and encouraging participation by minority and disadvantaged persons in technological innovation.

Program Conduct. Participating agencies conduct SBIR programs by reserving 1.25 percent of their extramural research and development budgets for funding agreements with small business concerns for R/R&D during the first two phases of the three-phase process described below. Each agency, at its sole discretion, selects the technical topics and subtopics included in its Solicitation, chooses its SBIR awardees, and may decide to make several awards or no awards under any subtopic.

Funding Agreements. The funding agreements used by NASA in both Phase I and Phase II programs are contracts rather than grants or cooperative agreements. All contract awards are subject to the availability of Federal government funds.

1.3 Three-Phase SBIR Program

Phase I. Project objectives in Phase I are to establish the feasibility and merit of an innovative scientific or technical concept proposed in response to an opportunity or agency need stated in a subtopic of this

Solicitation. Projects may be experimental or theoretical in nature. Concepts proposed must be useful to NASA and should also suggest either direct or indirect commercial applications of end results (potential Phase III pursuits).

To reduce the time and cost for small firms in preparing a responsive proposal under this Solicitation, **the entire Phase I proposal is limited to 25 8½ x 11 inch pages, including all forms and any attachments or enclosures.**

The proposal should concentrate on means to establish or demonstrate the scientific or technical feasibility of the proposed innovation to justify further NASA support in Phase II.

Evaluation and selection criteria, which are described in Section 4.1 of this Solicitation, concentrate on technical merit and innovativeness, value to NASA and to the economy, and the ability of the proposer to conduct the research.

Phase I funding agreements with NASA are fixed-price contract awards. Simplified contract documentation is employed. Price competition is not usually a factor in Phase I within the $50,000 funding limitation, since the basis of selection among the best proposals will be value to the government in terms of the stated evaluation criteria and NASA priorities. NASA alone is responsible for those determinations.

Successful offerors will have up to six months to complete their Phase I research and an additional 30 days in which to submit their Phase I final reports. Phase I contractors competing for Phase II must meet the Phase II proposal schedule provided by the NASA Installation requesting their Phase II proposals. The Phase I final report is required to accompany the Phase II proposal because of its importance in Phase II evaluations.

Phase II. This SBIR phase is the principal research effort. Its purpose is to continue the development of the most promising innovations among the Phase I projects in an effort to achieve results most useful to NASA at their completion and which, it is hoped, may have even more far reaching values to the economy. Competition for Phase II continuations is limited to Phase I performers satisfactorily completing Phase I projects who meet all SBIR eligibility requirements and from whom NASA Installations have requested Phase II proposals. Phase II awards are expected to be made during 1991 to continue projects whose Phase I results suggest highest technical feasibility, merit, and NASA priority. Phase II award funding may be for as much as $500,000. Phase II periods of performance do not usually exceed 24 months.

Phase II proposals are more comprehensive than those required for Phase I and are not page-limited. They are prepared in accordance with instructions provided by the contracting NASA Field Installations after the Phase I contracts are awarded.

Selection criteria for Phase II awards are similar to those for Phase I and are described in Section 4.2 of this Solicitation. They in addition include evaluations of the results of the Phase I project and contractor performance. Proposed Phase II cost is an unscored selection factor based on NASA's judgments of cost-value and reasonableness. Selections also depend on NASA program priorities and availability of funds.

Among Phase II proposals determined to be suitable for award and to have essentially equal merit, NASA will give special consideration to those which have obtained valid non-Federal funding commitments for Phase III activities. The Phase III commitment is described in Section 4.2-c of this Solicitation.

Phase III. This activity consists of (1) the privately financed pursuit of commercial applications of the results of SBIR Phase I and Phase II research, or (2) continued Federal Government support of the research or acquisition of end products for government use, or a combination of (1) and (2) where appropriate. SBIR set-aside funds will not be used to support Phase III activities. Offerors are encouraged to seek non-Federal funding commitments (see Solicitation Section 4.2.c) and to secure them prior to NASA's completion of Phase II proposal evaluations, since such commitments can be key considerations in Phase II selections for award. Further details on Phase III commitments will be provided to those selected for Phase I awards.

1.4 Eligibility To Participate in SBIR

Small Business. Only firms qualifying as small businesses as defined in Section 2.2 of this Solicitation are eligible to participate in the SBIR program. SBIR eligibility does not require that the offeror qualify as a minority and disadvantaged small business (see Section 2.3) or as a women-owned small business (see Section 2.4).

Place of Performance. For both Phase I and II, the R/R&D must be performed in the United States (see Section 2.5), unless specifically approved otherwise by NASA.

Principal Investigator. The Principal Investigator (PI) is always presumed to be key to the success of an SBIR project. Due to the central role of the PI in a project, Co-Principal Investigators are not acceptable to NASA. The PI must possess the requisite technical competence and authority to plan and guide the proposed research, must make a substantial contribution to its conduct if the project is selected for award and in fact perform the activities specified and provide the time committed in the proposal for that effort. After an award is made, any substitution for an approved Principal Investigator may be made only with NASA's consent.

The primary employment of the principal investigator must be with the small business firm at the time of contract award and during the conduct of the proposed research. Primary employment means that more than one-half of the principal investigator's time is spent in the employ of the small business. Primary employment with the small business precludes full-time employment or full-time student status in an academic institution during the conduct of the SBIR project. If a principal investigator is employed by an academic institution in a tenured position or on a tenure track, he or she is considered a full-time employee of that institution regardless of consulting, part-time or summer employment. Leaves of absence, sabbaticals, or other release time from an academic institution will not influence the determination of primary employment status unless the periods of such release are for the full Phase I and Phase II periods of performance.

If the primary employment of a principal investigator is not clear, NASA may require verification by the current employing institution before a proposal is accepted for evaluation and/or before an award is made. Should appropriate verification not be provided, such a proposal would be considered nonresponsive to this solicitation and would be returned to the proposer without evaluation or award.

1.5 General Information

Relevance of the Proposed Innovation. Each proposal must be based on an innovative, original concept relevant to meeting a NASA program need or opportunity identified in a subtopic listed in Appendix E of this Solicitation, and it may be submitted under only one subtopic (see Section 5.14-d). Proposals must conform to the format and requirements described in Section 3 of this Solicitation.

Questions about this Solicitation. For competitive fairness to all offerors, all communications regarding this Solicitation during the Phase I proposal preparation period are restricted to requests for clarification of solicitation instructions. Inquiries must be submitted in writing to the address below:

Mr. John A. Glaab
SBIR Program Manager
Code CR
National Aeronautics and
Space Administration
Washington, DC 20546

Attn: 90-1 Question

Additional Copies of this Solicitation or of Appendix A and B forms may be ordered by writing the SBIR Program Manager at the address listed above. Telephone requests will not be accepted.

Questions Regarding Proposal Status. Evaluation and selection of proposals for contract award will require approximately three months. No information on proposal status will be available until the final selections are announced, except for NASA's postal confirmation of receipt of proposal as noted in Section 6.5 of this Solicitation.

General Questions about the SBIR Program. Questions about NASA's SBIR Program which do not pertain to this Solicitation or requests for copies of the Solicitation may be submitted in writing to either Harry W. Johnson, SBIR Director, or John A. Glaab, SBIR Program Manager, at the above address or the offeror may call the SBIR

Program Inquiry telephone number, 202-453-2649, giving (1) company name; (2) full 1990 proposal number (example: NASA 90-1-04.06-9876A); (3) company address and telephone number; (4) whom to contact; (5) date and time the call placed to NASA; and (6) the specific inquiry.

Scientific and Technical Information. Information sources on NASA R/R&D programs include NASA Industrial Application Centers and the National Technical Information Service. Their addresses are included in Section 7.0 of this Solicitation. **NASA assumes no responsibility for any information these organizations may provide as interpretations of the content or intent of technical subtopics in this Solicitation, or for their assistance to offerors on proposals.**

2.0 DEFINITIONS

The following definitions apply for purposes of this Solicitation:

2.1 Research or Research and Development (R/R&D) – Any activity that is (1) a systematic, intensive study directed toward greater knowledge or understanding of the subject studied, (2) a systematic study directed specifically toward applying new knowledge to meet a recognized need, or (3) a systematic application of knowledge toward the production of useful materials, devices, and systems or methods, including the design, development, and improvement of prototypes and new processes to meet specific requirements.

2.2 Small Business – A concern that, at the time of award of Phase I and Phase II –

- Is independently owned and operated, is organized for profit, is not dominant in the field of operation in which it is proposing, and has its principal place of business located in the United States;
- Is at least 51 percent owned, or, in the case of a publicly owned business, at least 51 percent of its voting stock is owned by United States citizens or lawfully admitted permanent resident aliens; and
- Has, including its affiliates, a number of employees not exceeding 500 and meets the other regulatory requirements found in 13 CFR Part 121. Business concerns, other than investment companies licensed, or state development companies qualifying under the Small Business Investment Act of 1958, 15 U.S.C. 661, et seq., are affiliates of one another when, either directly or indirectly, (1) one concern controls or has the power to control the other or (2) a third party controls or has the power to control both. Control can be exercised through common ownership, common management, and contractual relationships. The term "affiliates" is defined in greater detail in 13 CFR 121.3(a). The term "number of employees" is defined in 13 CFR 121.2(b). Business concerns include, but are not limited to, a sole proprietorship, partnership, corporation, joint venture, association or cooperative.

2.3 Minority and Disadvantaged Small Business Concern – A small business concern that (1) is at least 51 percent owned by one or more individuals who are both socially and economically disadvantaged, or a publicly owned business having at least 51 percent of its stock owned by one or more socially and economically disadvantaged individuals, and (2) has its management and daily business controlled by one or more such individuals.

Minority and disadvantaged individuals include members of any of the following groups: Black Americans; Hispanic Americans; Native Americans (American Indians, Eskimos, Aleuts, and native Hawaiians); Asian-Pacific Americans; and subcontinent Asian Americans.

2.4 Women-Owned Small Business – A small business that is at least 51 percent owned by a woman or women who also control and operate it. To "control", in this context, means to exercise the power to make policy decisions. To "operate", in this context, means to be actively involved in day-to-day management.

2.5 United States – The 50 states, the District of Columbia, the Territories and possessions of the United States, the Commonwealth of Puerto Rico, the Commonwealth of the Northern Mariana

Islands, and the Trust Territory of the Pacific Islands.

2.6 Subcontract – Any agreement, other than one involving an employer-employee relationship, entered into by a Federal Government contractor calling for supplies or services required solely for the performance of the original contract. See also Sections 3.3.D-9 and 5.12 of this Solicitation.

2.7 Innovation Research – R/R&D on an innovation. Innovation in the context of the NASA SBIR program includes, but is not limited to, invention. Innovation encompasses new, original and imaginative approaches to the solution of new and old problems, evolutionary and revolutionary improvements or advances to existing technology, exploitation of new technological opportunities, and some limited aspects of basic research when such objectives are stated in the technical subtopics.

Proposals for surveys, general or specific studies, and conventional applications of engineering design, development or testing of products which do not require innovation as defined above will not be evaluated in the SBIR program. NASA would expect to procure such activities and products through other means.

3.0 PHASE I PROPOSAL CONTENT AND PREPARATION

3.1 Proposal Objectives and Considerations

The purpose of a Phase I proposal under the SBIR Program is to provide sufficient information to persuade NASA that the proposed work represents a sound approach to the investigation of an important scientific or engineering innovation of interest to NASA and is worthy of support under the stated selection criteria. A proposal should be self-contained and written with the care and thoroughness accorded papers for publication.

Important considerations include the following:

- SBIR proposals must be limited to activities requiring significant scientific or technical innovation R/R&D, either experimental or theoretical. They may or may not involve construction and evaluation of a laboratory prototype, but **each project must develop specific end products or results** for delivery at the conclusion of the project which may include data, reports, hardware and software programs.
- Scientific or technical merit of the proposed innovation and its value to the NASA program are primary factors without which no award would be made.
- An SBIR proposal may respond to only one of the subtopics in Appendix E, (see Section 5.14-d) and must address a NASA program objective or opportunity described therein. Ideally, the proposed innovation should also serve as the basis, directly or indirectly, for new commercial products, processes, or services which may benefit the general economy.
- Proposals directed toward market research or the commercial development of existing products or concepts - unproven, proven, proprietary, patented or otherwise – should not be submitted for SBIR support. Such activities are considered responsibilities of the private sector and may not be funded by SBIR.

3.2 General Requirements

Page Limitation. A Phase I SBIR proposal shall not exceed a total of 25 standard 8-1/2" x 11" pages consisting of the cover page (Appendix A form in this Solicitation), project summary (Appendix B form in this Solicitation), the technical proposal, the proposed budget (Appendix C form in this Solicitation), and any enclosures, attachments or addendum the offeror provides. Each page shall be numbered consecutively at the center, bottom. All material supplied, except the check list (Appendix D in this Solicition) will be included in the page count. **Proposals exceeding the 25 page limitation will be returned without consideration.**

Type Size. No type size smaller than elite is to be used for text or tables, except as legends on reduced drawings. Pages are to be printed on one side only, and may be single or double spaced.

Brevity is Desired. The proposal should be direct, concise, and informative. Promotional and non-project-related material should not be included. **Offerors are requested not to use the entire 25 page allowance unless that is actually necessary. Appropriate brevity facilitates proposal evaluations.**

Content and Format. All required items of information are to be covered fully and in the order set forth in Section 3.3 of this Solicitation, but the space allocated to each will depend on the project chosen and the Principal Investigator's approach.

NASA Use of Optical Character Readers. To facilitate proposal processing, NASA intends to employ optical character readers to record proposal cover sheet and project summary information wherever possible. Therefore it is required that the proposal cover sheet (Appendix A) and the project summary (Appendix B) be typed carefully on the indicated lines using one of the following type styles:

COURIER 12 10 or 12 PITCH
COURIER 72 10 PITCH
ELITE 72
LETTER GOTHIC 10 or 12 PITCH
OCR-B 10 or 12 PITCH
PICA 72 10 PITCH
PRESTIGE ELITE 10 or 12 PITCH
PRESTIGE PICA 10 PITCH

IMPORTANT: Do Not Use Proportional Spacing on Appendixes A and B

Check List. The Check List (Appendix D in this Solicitation) is provided to assist the offeror. One copy of Appendix D is to be completed and included with the original signed copies of Appendixes A and B as noted in Section 6.1 of this Solicitation. The Check List is not counted as a proposal page.

3.3 Required Phase I Proposal Format

The format required for all Phase I proposals is provided herewith. **Proposals will consist of Parts A, B, C, D and E** below, but may also include supplementary information (included in the total page count) at the option of the offeror. **Part D** is further subdivided into eleven numbered Sections. **All proposal Parts and Sections must be addressed, and must follow in order.**

Part A. Cover Sheet. The offeror shall include a photocopy of the signed original cover sheet (Appendix A in this Solicitation) as page 1 of each copy of the proposal. No other cover sheet is permitted. The proposal title must be concise and descriptive, but must not be stated as an acronym.

Part B. Project Summary. The offeror shall include a photocopy of the signed original project summary (Appendix B in this Solicitation) as page 2 of each copy of the proposal. The technical abstract section should include (1) a brief description of the **proposed innovation** and how it addresses the stated subtopic problem or opportunity, (2) the project objectives, and (3) a description of the effort proposed and results anticipated. In summarizing anticipated results, the expected NASA applications and benefits and any potential commercial applications shall be identified. **The project summary of successful proposals will be published by NASA, therefore ALL information provided on Appendix B of all proposals will be treated by NASA as non-proprietary information.**

Part C. Table of Contents. Page 3 of the proposal shall begin with a brief table of contents indicating the presence and page numbers of each of the parts and sections of the proposal.

NOTE: Detailed instructions for completing Appendixes A, B and C are printed on their reverse sides.

Part D. Technical Proposal. The Technical Proposal shall consist of the following **eleven sections. Entries are required in each section.**

Sect. 1. Identification and Significance of the Innovation. The first paragraph shall contain a clear and succinct statement of **the specific innovation** proposed, why it is an innovation, and how it is relevant and important to meeting the need or opportunity described in the subtopic. The paragraph shall contain no more than 150 words. **NASA reserves the right to refuse proposals which lack this introductory paragraph.**

This section of the proposal may also include appropriate background and elaboration to explain the proposed innovation and its value to NASA.

Sect. 2. Phase I Technical Objectives. This section shall include the specific objectives of the Phase I effort and state the technical questions the offeror will try to answer to determine the feasibility of the proposed innovation.

Sect. 3. Phase I Work Plan. This section should be comprehensive and explanatory, normally constituting approximately one-third of the total proposal. It shall include a detailed description of the proposed Phase I activities indicating what will be done and where the work will be carried out. The methods planned to achieve each objective or task should be discussed in detail. Schedules (Gantt Charts or other suitable scheduled task displays), task descriptions and assignments, resource allocations and planned accomplishments including project milestones shall be included.

The Phase I Work Plan must be complete and self-contained. However, Section 5.4-a of this Solicitation gives instructions for including proprietary information in an SBIR proposal as a separate "Proprietary Addendum," and what must be done to protect such information from public disclosure. Offerors are advised to avoid including proprietary information if at all possible.

Sect. 4. Related R/R&D and Bibliography of Related Work. The purpose of this section is to make clear the offeror's awareness of key recent developments by others in the specific subject area. It should include any significant R/R&D directly related to the proposal that was conducted by the Principal Investigator or by the offeror's firm. Any planned coordination with outside sources during the course of the proposed research should also be stated.

At the offeror's option, this section may include concise bibliographic references in support of the proposal if they are confined to activities directly related to the proposed work.

Sect. 5. Relationship with Phase II or other Future R/R&D. This section shall explain why the expected Phase I results should warrant Phase II continuation, state the anticipated Phase II objectives, and include the offeror's suggested applications by NASA. Any other planned R/R&D related to the proposed research should also be noted.

Sect. 6. Potential Commercial Applications. Commercialization of the results of research innovations supported by Federal R&D is an important SBIR goal. Offerors shall discuss whether the results or products of their proposed innovation research have potential direct or indirect commercial applications, and include their intentions (and plans, if any) to pursue commercialization in Phase III if the research effort through Phase II is successful.

Sect. 7. Company Information. This section will provide information needed by evaluators to assess the ability of the firm to carry out the proposed Phase I and projected Phase II activities. While extensive background or experience is not a prerequisite for an SBIR award, the ability of the offeror to perform the proposed activities must be established before an award is made.

A description of the firm's business organization, operations, R/R&D capabilities and experience is to be provided if it has such a history. All firms, including start-up firms are requested to outline their business objectives or plans in which this SBIR project would fit.

This section must also provide a description of the firm's physical facilities including any instrumentation and equipment pertinent to the proposed research. If facilities, equipment and instrumentation needed for the proposed research are not presently available, the offeror must explain how they are to be obtained.

As a general rule, NASA will not fund the purchase of equipment or instrumentation (or acquisition of facilities) under SBIR Phase I contracts. If such purchases are authorized, title will vest in the U.S. government. Refer also to Part E, below.

Sect. 8. Key Company Personnel. This Section shall identify the key company employees to be committed to Phase I activities, including the Principal Investigator and other individuals whose expertise is essential to the success of the research. Information on their education and experience, and directly related bibliographic information is required. Offerors are requested to avoid extensive vitae and publication lists not pertinent to the proposed research.

This section shall also establish the Principal Investigator's eligibility (see Section 1.4 of this Solicitation) and indicate the extent to which (1) other proposals recently submitted or planned to be submitted in 1990, and (2) existing projects for which he/she is identified as PI would commit his/her time concurrently with this proposed activity.

Sect. 9. Subcontracts and Consultants. Up to one-third of the research and/or analytical effort in Phase I may be conducted under subcontract to other firms, nonprofit organizations and individual consultants (see Section 5.12 of this Solicitation). Subcontracting is encouraged when it permits the firm to write a better proposal, conduct more valuable research, and improve its prospects for commercial success.

This section must describe any subcontracting requirements and identify the organizations and individuals with whom subcontracts are planned. Generally, these arrangements will be viewed as key to the success of the work, so the expertise to be subcontracted must be described in detail as well as the functions, services, time intervals and extent of effort to be provided.

The proposal must include an agreement by each subcontracting organization and individual consultant that they will be available at the times required for the purposes and extent of effort described in the proposal.

Sect. 10. Related Proposals to and Awards from Other Agencies. If the offeror (a) has received Federal government awards for related work, or (b) has submitted proposals for essentially equivalent or similar work under other Federal government program solicitations, or (c) intends to submit proposals for such work to other agencies during 1990, those awards, proposals and intentions shall be identified. A statement must be included indicating:

(1) The agencies to which proposals were submitted or from which awards were received.

(2) Date of proposal submission or date of award.

(3) Solicitation numbers under which proposals were submitted or awards received.

(4) The specific research topic for each proposal submitted or awards received.

(5) Titles of research projects.

(6) Name and title of principal investigator for each proposal submitted or award received.

(7) Intended proposal submissions in 1990.

NOTE: If no such awards have been received, or proposals submitted or intended, the offeror shall so state.

Sect. 11. Previous NASA SBIR Awards Received. Offerors who have received previous NASA SBIR awards shall provide a list including contract numbers and titles, indicating the year of award and the NASA installation making the award. If no NASA awards have been received, the offeror shall so state.

Part E. Proposed Budget. Offerors shall complete Appendix C, SBIR Summary Budget, and include it (and any budget explanation sheets if needed) as the last page(s) of the proposal. Items on Appendix C that do not apply to the proposed project may be omitted. What matters is that enough information be available to allow NASA to understand how the offeror plans to use the requested funds and business-like evidence that the proposed budget is realistic and cost-effective. Special attention is directed to the following items:

Title to All Property. Because NASA will not normally fund instrumentation, equipment or facility acquisition under Phase I, the inclusion of such items should be avoided if possible and must be fully justified if included. Any inclusion of such items will be carefully reviewed relative to need and appropriateness for the research proposed.

Equipment is defined as an article of non-expendable, tangible, personal property having a useful life of more than one year and an acquisition cost of $1,000 or more per unit. Title to all property (including equipment) acquired under an SBIR contract will be vested in NASA unless it is determined that transfer of title to the contractor would be more cost effective than recovery of the property by NASA.

It should be noted that prototypes, working models and devices, measurement instrumentation and test apparatus built under NASA SBIR contracts and which cost more than $1000 per unit to develop are normally considered to be equipment owned by and deliverable to NASA. Proposals should clarify the Offeror's expectations or plans, if any, for future use and possible ownership of such items to avoid possible future misunderstandings.

Travel. Budgets for travel funds are not normally acceptable, but if proposed must be justified as essential to the conduct of the project.

Profit. A profit or fee may be included in the proposed budget as noted in Solicitation Section 5.9.

4.0 PROPOSAL EVALUATION AND AWARD SELECTION

4.1 Phase I

a. Evaluation and Selection. The initial step is screening for compliance with administrative requirements of the Solicitation. Proposals which pass that screening are then reviewed to determine whether they respond to the subtopic chosen by the offeror. Those found to be responsive are evaluated in greater depth by two or more scientists and engineers at the NASA Installation responsible for the research, using the criteria listed below.

Evaluators base their conclusions only on information contained in the proposal. Offerors should not assume that evaluators are acquainted with the firm or key individuals or with any experiments or other information referred to but not described in referenced professional journals. To be of any value in this process, relevant information must be identified in Part D-4 of the proposal.

Each proposal is judged and scored on its own merits using an established uniform scoring procedure, then is ranked relative to all others evaluated under the same subtopic. Those considered suitable for selection are recommended for further consideration by the NASA Installation SBIR Committee, which prepares final recommendations for selection in priority order, based on proposal merit, program balance and Installation needs. These recommendations are then forwarded to NASA Headquarters for final selection decisions which take into consideration the recommendations from all Installations and overall NASA priorities and program balance. Proposals judged to have the highest merit and value to NASA will be selected for negotiations that may lead to contract awards.

Proposals are evaluated at the NASA Installation cited in the Solicitation subtopic, but other NASA Installations may also conduct evaluations and make recommendations for selections of any proposals received by NASA from this Solicitation.

In the evaluation and handling of proposals, NASA will make every effort to protect the confidentiality of the proposals and their evaluations.

b. Phase I Evaluation Criteria. NASA plans to select proposals which offer the best value to the Government, giving approximately equal consideration to each of the following four criteria except for the first, which has twice the weight of each other item:

1. **Scientific/technical merit** of (a) the proposed innovation and its relevance to the needs stated in the selected subtopic, and (b) the proposal's statement of objectives and approach for addressing questions of feasibility. Special emphasis is placed on innovativeness and originality.

2. **Qualifications** of the principal investigator, other key staff, consultants and subcontractors, if any, and the adequacy of available or obtainable instrumentation and facilities.

3. Anticipated benefits (technical and/or economic) to the NASA mission through applications subsequent to Phase II, and the potential for direct or derived commercial applications of the expected results or products if the research is successful.

4. Soundness and technical merit of the proposed work plan including its likelihood of meeting the Phase I objective of establishing the feasibility and merit of the proposed innovation as a basis for Phase II continuation.

4.2 Phase II

During the course of Phase I, the NASA Installations awarding SBIR Phase I contracts will issue requests for Phase II proposals to those contractors whose progress is deemed to be satisfactory, if NASA is interested in Phase II continuations. A Phase II proposal may be submitted only by the firm performing the Phase I research. Information provided by NASA will include instructions regarding Phase II proposal submission, the relative importance of the evaluation factors to be employed, the date when Phase II proposals must be submitted (usually, one month after the end of the Phase I performance period), and other information to facilitate their compliance with Phase II requirements.

a. Evaluation and Selection. Phase II proposals undergo a technical review and competitive selection process in greater depth than Phase I proposals. As in Phase I, the Phase II proposals are evaluated by the NASA Installations responsible for the research using uniform evaluation procedures and the criteria noted below. Proposals are then ranked by the Installation SBIR Committee taking into consideration overall quality, value to NASA, and Installation program balance. Recommendations are forwarded to NASA Headquarters for final consideration with the recommendations made by all Installations.

Final selections take into consideration overall NASA programmatic or schedule requirements and availability of funds. Special consideration is given to acceptable proposals of essentially equivalent merit for which valid non-Federal funding commitments for Phase III activities have been obtained (refer to Section 4.2.c of this Solicitation).

At its discretion NASA may initiate early negotiations for a Phase II award at any time after the proposal has been received.

b. Phase II Evaluation Criteria. Evaluation criteria for Phase II proposals include:

1. Scientific/technical merit and feasibility of the proposed R&D, with special emphasis on its innovativeness, originality and technical payoff potential if successful.

2. Results of Phase I, including feasibility of the innovation and how well the results support current NASA program priorities.

3. Future importance and eventual value of the product, process or technology results to the mission of NASA after completion of Phase II. The potential for commercial applications of the expected research results or products if the research is successful will also be considered.

4. Ability of the Small Firm. NASA will assess the ability of the firm to conduct Phase II based on (a) the validity of the project plans for achieving the stated goals, (b) the qualifications and ability of the project team (Principal Investigator, company staff, consultants and subcontractors) relative to the proposed research, and (c) the availability of any required equipment and facilities.

c. Non-Federal Commitments for Phase III Funding. Valid non-Federal capital commitments for Phase III follow-on activities may be contingent on the outcome of Phase II and on other stated circumstances, but must provide that a specific, substantial amount (usually at least half the Phase II funding request) will be made available to the firm to pursue Phase III and must indicate the source and date or conditions under which the funds will be made available. Realistic, substantial self-commitments by the firm can also qualify.

Valid commitments must be provided as brief letters to the proposing firms from the organization making the commitments. Preferably, they should accompany the Phase II proposal but they may be considered up until final Phase II award decisions have been made by NASA. It should be noted that mere expressions of technical interest in the outcome of the Phase II research, or of potential future financial interest by a third party are not valid Phase III commitments and will not be accepted as such by NASA.

4.3 Debriefing of Unsuccessful Offerors

After final Phase I and Phase II award decisions have been announced, a critique (a debriefing) for an unsuccessful offeror may be provided – to the offeror only – upon written request. Telephone requests for debriefings will not be accepted. Debriefings are not opportunities to reopen selection decisions. They are intended to acquaint the offeror with perceived strengths and weaknesses of the proposal and perhaps to provide suggestions for constructive future action by the offeror.

Debriefings will not disclose the identity of the proposal evaluators and NASA will provide the evaluators' actual comments in the course of debriefings only at its option. Such information is exempt from Freedom of Information disclosure, as are proposal scores, proposal rankings in the competition, and the content of and comparisons with other proposals with which they were in competition.

Phase I. For Phase I proposals, all requests for debriefing must be directed in writing to the SBIR Program Manager, NASA Headquarters, within 45 days after notification has been mailed to the offeror that its proposal was not selected for award. When feasible to do so, oral (telephone) debriefings will be provided; otherwise written debriefing comments will be mailed.

Phase II. To request debriefings on Phase II proposals, proposers must contact the SBIR Procurement Officer at the NASA Installation responsible for their Phase I contract.

5.0 CONSIDERATIONS

5.1 Awards

In October 1990, NASA expects to announce the selection of approximately 275 proposals for negotiation of fixed-price Phase I contracts with values ranging up to $50,000. Following contract negotiations and awards, Phase I contractors will usually have six months to carry out their proposed Phase I programs.

For planning purposes, NASA anticipates that during 1991 approximately 50 percent of the Phase I projects resulting from this Solicitation may be selected for Phase II continuations, based on the results of Phase I activities and competitive evaluations of Phase II proposals. Phase II funding agreements may be either fixed-price type or cost-type contracts. Phase II performance periods normally will not exceed 24 months with funding not exceeding $500,000.

Both Phase I and Phase II awards are subject to availability of funds. NASA has no obligation to make any specific number of Phase I or Phase II awards based on this Solicitation, and may elect to make several or no awards in any specific technical topic or subtopic.

5.2 Reports

Six (original plus five) copies of a final report on the Phase I project must be submitted to NASA within 30 days after completion of the Phase I research effort. The final report shall include a single page project summary as the first page, on a form to be provided by NASA for that purpose, identifying the purpose of the research, a brief description of the research carried out, the research findings or results including the degree to which the Phase I objectives were achieved, and whether the results justify Phase II continuation. The potential applications of the project results through Phase II both for NASA purposes and for commercial purposes will also be included. The project summary is to be submitted without restriction for NASA publication. The balance of the report shall elaborate the project objectives, work carried out, results obtained, and assessments of technical feasibility. Rights to this data shall be in accordance with the policies set forth in Section 5.5.

To avoid duplication of effort, language used in the Phase I report may be used verbatim in the Phase II proposal.

5.3 Payment Schedule

Payments on Phase I contracts may be invoiced as follows: one-third at the time of award, one-third at project mid-point after award, and the remainder upon acceptance of the final report by NASA. Payments will be made 30 days after receipt of valid invoices.

5.4 Treatment and Protection of Proposal Information

a. Proprietary Information. It is NASA policy to use information (data) included in proposals for evaluation purposes only and to protect such information from unauthorized use or disclosure. While this policy does not require that the proposal bear a notice, protection can be assured only to the extent that an appropriate "Notice", set forth in the clause of the NASA FAR Supplement at 18-52.215-72, Restriction on Use and Disclosure of Proposal and Quotation Information (Data), is applied to the data which constitute trade secrets or other information that is commercial or financial and confidential or privileged, as follows:

> "NOTICE: No proprietary information is included except in a Proprietary Addendum. The information (data) on pages _________ in the Proprietary Addendum Section of this proposal constitute a trade secret and/or information that is commercial or financial and confidential or privileged. It is furnished to the Government in confidence with the understanding that it will not, without permission of the offeror, be used or disclosed other than for evaluation purposes; provided, however, in the event a contract is awarded on this proposal, the Government may obtain additional rights to use and disclose this information (data)."

Other information will be afforded protection to the extent permitted by law, but NASA assumes no liability for use and disclosure of information to which the "Notice" has not been appropriately applied.

The offerer should also note that the above notice is printed on the proposal cover page to alert NASA to the presence of a "Proprietary Addendum" if one is included. **Proposals containing any other information marked as proprietary will not be evaluated.**

b. Non-NASA Reviewers. In addition to Government personnel, NASA, at its discretion and in accordance with 18-15.413-2 of the NASA FAR Supplement, may utilize scientists and engineers from outside the government in the proposal review process. Any decision to obtain outside evaluation shall take into consideration requirements for the avoidance of organizational or personal conflicts of interest and the competitive relationship, if any, between the prospective contractor or subcontractor(s) and the prospective outside evaluator. Any such evaluation will be under agreement with the evaluator that the information (data) contained in the proposal will be used only for evaluation purposes and will not be further disclosed.

c. Release of Proposal Information. By submission of a proposal, the offeror agrees to permit the government to disclose publicly the information contained in Appendixes A and B. Other proposal information (data) is considered to be the property of the offeror, and NASA will protect it from public disclosure to the extent permitted by law.

It is NASA's practice to notify the offeror of the proposal before releasing any information (data) contained therein pursuant to a request under the Freedom of Information Act (5 U.S.C. 552) and, time permitting, to consult with the offeror to obtain assistance in determining the eligibility of the information (data) in question as an exemption under the Act.

d. Final Disposition of Proposals. The government retains ownership of the copies of proposals accepted for evaluation and they will not be returned to the offeror.

Copies of all proposals evaluated will be retained until the Phase I selection awards have been made, after which time those which were not selected for award will be destroyed.

5.5 Rights in Data Developed Under SBIR Contracts

Rights to data used in, or first produced under, any Phase I or Phase II contract are specified in the clause at FAR 52.227-20, Rights in Data - SBIR Program. Such clause provides for rights consistent with the following:

a. Some data of a general nature are to be furnished to NASA without restriction (i.e., with unlimited rights) and may be published by NASA. These data will normally be limited to the project summary accompanying any periodic progress reports and the final report required to be submitted (see Section 5.2) but, in any event, the requirement for them will be specifically set forth in any contract resulting from this solicitation.

b. In keeping with NASA's policy, data that constitute trade secrets or other information that is commercial or financial and confidential or privileged **and developed at private expense** will not normally be acquired, but if acquired will be with "limited rights" or "restricted rights." Such rights do not include the right to use the data for manufacturing or reprocurement purposes.

c. Other than as required by (a) above, rights in technical data including software developed under the terms of any funding agreement resulting from proposals submitted in response to this Solicitation shall remain with the contractor, except that the government shall have the limited right to use such data for government purposes and shall not release such data outside the government without permission of the contractor for a period of two years from completion of the project from which the data were generated, i.e., after completion of Phase II if the Phase I project receives Phase II funding. However, effective at the conclusion of the two year period, the government shall retain a royalty-free license for government use of any technical data delivered under an SBIR contract whether patented or not, but (except per (b) above) is relieved of all disclosure prohibitions and assumes no liability for unauthorized use of the data by third parties.

5.6 Copyrights

Contractors will be permitted (in accordance with paragraph (c) of the clause at FAR 52.227-20) to assert or establish claim to copyright data first produced under a Phase I or Phase II contract, subject to a paid-up, non-exclusive, irrevocable, worldwide license for governmental purposes. The contractor is required to include an appropriate credit line acknowledging government support for any works published under copyrights.

5.7 Patents

The contractor will, as provided in the clause at FAR 52.227-11, Patent Rights - Retention by Contractor (Short Form), have first option to retain title to inventions made in the performance of any Phase I or Phase II contract in accordance with P.L. 96-517 (35 U.S.C. 200, et. seq.). This option is subject to the reservations and limitations, including a nonexclusive, royalty-free, irrevocable license in the Government and certain march-in rights to assure commercialization, as required by 35 U.S.C. 203 and implementing regulations thereunder.

Whenever an invention is made and reported under any NASA contract, it is NASA policy to withhold such report from disclosure to the public and to use reasonable efforts to withhold other information which may disclose the invention (provided that NASA is notified of the information and the invention to which it relates) for a reasonable time to allow the contractor to obtain patent protection as authorized by 35 U.S.C. 205.

5.8 Cost Sharing

Cost sharing is permitted for proposals under this Program Solicitation. However, cost sharing is not required, nor will it be a factor in proposal evaluation. NASA limits the Phase I award amount to $50,000.

5.9 Profit or Fee

Both Phase I and Phase II SBIR contracts may include a reasonable profit or fee.

5.10 Joint Ventures and Limited Partnerships

Both joint ventures and limited partnerships are permitted, provided the entity created qualifies as a small business in accordance with the definition in Section 2.2.

5.11 Similar Proposals and Prior Work

Submission of related proposals to and receipt of related awards from other agencies, intentions to submit related proposals during to 1990 to other agencies, and prior NASA SBIR awards received by the offeror must be identified in the Technical Proposal Sections D-10 and D-11 as noted in Section 3.3 of this Solicitation.

If an award is made pursuant to a proposal submitted under this Program Solicitation, the firm will be required to certify that it has not previously been, nor is currently being, paid for essentially equivalent work by any agency of the Federal government.

5.12 Limits on Subcontracting Research and Analytical Work

Subcontracts (defined in Section 2.6 of this Solicitation) may be placed with other firms, universities and other non-profit organizations, and with individual consultants, but there are cost limits on subcontracting the research and analytical portions of both Phase I and Phase II contracts:

- For Phase I, a minimum of two-thirds of the research and/or analytical effort must be performed by the proposing firm unless otherwise approved in writing by the contracting officer.
- For Phase II, a minimum of one-half of the research and/or analytical effort must be performed by the proposing firm unless approved in writing by the contracting officer.

NOTE: The costs of research and analytical effort do not include the SBIR contractor's costs for overhead, general and administrative costs, and profit or fee.

5.13 Contractor Commitments

Upon award of a contract, the contractor will be required to make certain legal commitments through acceptance of numerous clauses in the Phase I contract. The outline that follows illustrates the types of clauses that will be included in the Phase I contract. This is not a complete list of clauses to be included in Phase I contracts, nor does it contain specific wording of these clauses. Copies of complete general provisions will be made available prior to award.

a. Standards of Work. Work performed under the contract must conform to high professional standards. Analyses, equipment, and components for use by NASA will require special consideration to satisfy the stringent safety and reliability requirements imposed in aerospace applications.

b. Inspection. Work performed under the contract is subject to government inspection and evaluation at all reasonable times.

c. Examination of Records. The Comptroller General (or a duly authorized representative) shall have the right to examine any directly pertinent records of the contractor involving transactions related to the contract.

d. Default. The government may terminate the contract if the contractor fails to perform the contracted work.

e. Termination for Convenience. The contract may be terminated at any time by the government if it deems termination to be in its best interest, in which case the contractor will be compensated for work performed and for reasonable termination costs.

f. Disputes. Any dispute concerning the contract that cannot be resolved by mutual agreement shall be decided by the contracting officer with right of appeal.

g. Contract Work Hours. The contractor may not require an employee to work more than 40 hours a week unless the employee is compensated accordingly (that is, receives overtime pay).

h. Equal Opportunity. The contractor will not discriminate against any employee or applicant for employment because of race, color, religion, sex or national origin.

i. Affirmative Action for Veterans. The contractor will not discriminate against any employee or applicant for employment because he or she is a disabled veteran or veteran of the Vietnam era.

j. Affirmative Action for Handicapped. The contractor will not discriminate against any employee or applicant for employment because he or she is physically or mentally handicapped.

k. Officials Not to Benefit. No member of or delegate to Congress shall benefit from the contract.

l. Covenant Against Contingent Fees. No person or agency has been employed to solicit or secure the contract upon an understanding for compensation except bona fide employees or commercial agencies maintained by the contractor for the purpose of securing business.

m. Gratuities. The contract may be terminated by the government if any gratuities have been offered to any representative of the government to secure the contract.

n. Patent Infringement. The contractor shall report to NASA each notice or claim of patent infringement based on the performance of the contract.

5.14 Additional Information

a. Precedence of Contract over Solicitation. This Program Solicitation is intended for informational purposes and reflects current planning. If there is any inconsistency between the information contained herein and the terms of any resulting SBIR contract, the terms of the contract are controlling.

b. Evidence of Contractor Responsibility. Before award of an SBIR contract, the Government may request the offeror to submit certain organizational, management, personnel, and financial information to establish responsibility of the offeror.

c. Limitations on Awards. This Solicitation is not an offer by the Government to make any specific number of awards under either Phase I or Phase II. NASA is not responsible for any monies expended by the offeror before award of any contract resulting from this Solicitation. Also, awards under this Program Solicitation 90-1 are contingent upon the availability of funds.

d. Multiple Proposal Submissions. An offeror may submit any number of different Phase I proposals on different subtopics, or different proposals on the same subtopic. However, every proposal must be limited in scope to one subtopic. Should the offeror consider a proposal to have relevance to more than one subtopic, the offeror must choose the one under which to submit the proposal. Neither an identical proposal nor substantially similar proposals may be submitted to the other subtopics. Within the submitted proposal, the discussion of the innovation may identify other subtopics for which the concept is believed relevant; **however, such identification will not insure that the proposal will be evaluated within any subtopic other than the one to which the proposal is addressed, or at NASA Installations other than those identified in the subtopic addressed.**

Offerors should be aware that none of any identical or substantially similar proposals submitted in response to this Solicitation, whether to one or to several subtopics, will be evaluated.

e. Classified Proposals. NASA will not accept classified proposals.

f. Unsolicited Proposals. Unsolicited proposals will not be accepted under the SBIR program in either Phase I or Phase II.

6.0 SUBMISSION OF PROPOSALS

6.1 What to Send

Offerors must submit the following items for each proposal:

a. One Original Proposal Cover as a separate sheet. This is Appendix A, a red-printed form included in this Solicitation.

b. One Original Project Summary as a separate sheet. This is Appendix B, a red-printed form included in this Solicitation.

c. One Check List as a separate sheet. This is Appendix D, a black-printed form included in this Solicitation.

NOTE: DO NOT STAPLE ITEMS (a), (b) and (c) TOGETHER: LEAVE SEPARATE.

d. Five black and white copies of the entire proposal, complete with copies of Appendices A, B and C (but excluding Appendix D) and any optional enclosures, attachments and addenda. Each proposal copy is to be stapled separately. All pages are included in the page count, which is limited to 25 standard 8-1/2" x 11" pages.

6.2 Physical Packaging Requirements

Bindings. Do not use bindings or special covers. Staple the pages of each copy of the proposal **only** in the upper left-hand corner.

Packaging. All items (6.1 a through d) for **any proposal must be sent in the same package.** If more than one proposal is being submitted, it is requested that all proposals be sent in the same package whenever possible.

NOTE: DO NOT SEND ADDITIONAL SETS of any proposal as "insurance" that they will be received.

6.3 Where to Send Proposals

Proposals shall be addressed as below:

SBIR Program Manager
Code CR
National Aeronautics and
Space Administration
Washington, DC 20546

Note: No street address is required

Handcarried proposals or proposals delivered by messenger should be delivered to the NASA Headquarters Mailroom, which address is Room A16, Federal Office Building 10B, NASA Headquarters, 600 Independence Avenue, SW, Washington, DC, 20546. Secure packaging is mandatory. NASA cannot process proposals damaged in transit.

NOTE: 1. Deliver packages only to NASA Headquarters.

2. Proposals cannot be received by NASA on Saturdays or Sundays or Federal holidays.

6.4 Deadline for Proposal Receipt

Deadline for receipt of Phase I proposals at NASA is 4:00 p.m., EDT, July 16, 1990. NASA assumes no responsibility for evaluating proposals received after the stated deadline. Offerors are cautioned to be careful of unforseen delays that can cause late arrival of proposals at NASA with the result that they may not be evaluated. Nevertheless, should such actions be deemed to be in the best interests of the government, NASA reserves the right to accept late proposals or modifications to otherwise acceptable proposals received before the stated deadline. Such acceptances would be made only under unusual and justifiable circumstances and when they would not provide unfair competitive advantages to the offerors.

6.5 Acknowledgement of Proposal Receipt

NASA will acknowledge receipt of proposals by a postal card mailed to the company official endorsing the proposal cover sheet. If a proposal acknowledgement card is not received from NASA within 30 days following the closing date of this Solicitation, the offeror should call 202-453-8702. **NASA will not accept telephone inquiries regarding receipt of proposals prior to August 15, 1990.**

6.6 Withdrawal of Proposals

Proposals may be withdrawn by written notice or telegram (including mailgram) received at any time before award. Proposals may be withdrawn in person by an offeror or an authorized representative, if the representative's identity is made known and the representative signs a receipt for the proposal.

7.0 SCIENTIFIC AND TECHNICAL INFORMATION SOURCES

The following organizations can provide technology search and/or document services and can be contacted directly for service and cost information.

National Technical Information Service
5285 Port Royal Road
Springfield, VA 22161
(703) 487-4600

Aerospace Research Applications Center
Indianapolis Center for Advanced Research
611 N. Capitol Avenue
Indianapolis, IN 46204
(317) 262-5003

Central Industrial Applications Center
Rural Enterprises, Inc.
P.O. Box 1335
Durant, OK 74702
(405) 924-6822

Southern Technology Applications Center
One Progress Boulevard
Box 24
Progress Center
Alachua, FL 32615
(904) 462-3913

NASA Industrial Applications Center
823 William Pitt Union
University of Pittsburgh
Pittsburgh, PA 15260
(412) 648-7010

NASA/UK Technology Applications Center
University of Kentucky
109 Kinkead Hall
Lexington, KY 40506-0057
(606) 257-6322

NERAC, Inc.
One Technology Drive
Tolland, CT 06084
(203) 872-7000

NASA Industrial Applications Center
University of Southern California
Research Annex
3716 S. Hope Street Rm 200
Los Angeles, CA 90007-4344
(213) 743-8988
Attention: Radford King

Technology Applications Center
2808 Central, S.E.
University of New Mexico
Albuquerque, NM 87131
(505) 277-3622

Computer Software Management and Information Center
382 East Broad Street
University of Georgia
Athens, GA 30602
(404) 542-3265

North Carolina Science and Technology Research Center
P.O. Box 12235
Research Triangle Park, NC 27709
(919) 549-0671

NASA/SU Industrial Applications Center
Southern University
P.O. Box 9737
Baton Rouge, LA 70813-9737
(504) 771-6272

8.0 TECHNICAL TOPICS

Proposals shall address subtopics in Appendix E under the following technical topics:

01.00 Aeronautical Propulsion and Power
02.00 Aerodynamics and Acoustics
03.00 Aircraft Systems, Subsystems, and Operations
04.00 Materials and Structures
05.00 Teleoperators and Robotics
06.00 Computer Sciences and Applications
07.00 Information Systems and Data Handling
08.00 Instrumentation and Sensors
09.00 Spacecraft Systems and Subsystems
10.00 Space Power
11.00 Space Propulsion
12.00 Human Habitability and Biology in Space
13.00 Quality Assurance, Safety, and Check-Out for Ground and Space Operations
14.00 Satellite and Space Systems Communications
15.00 Materials Processing, Micro-Gravity, and Commercial Applications in Space

APPENDIX A - PROPOSAL COVER

NATIONAL AERONAUTICS AND SPACE ADMINISTRATION

SBIR 90-1 SOLICITATION PROPOSAL COVER
(Instructions on Reverse Side)

PROPOSAL NUMBER
(TO BE COMPLETED BY PROPOSER)

	4 DIGIT SUBTOPIC NUMBER	LAST 4 DIGITS OF FIRM PHONE NO.	CHANGE LETTER
90-1	___ . ___	_____	_____

ENTER PROPOSAL NUMBER ON APPENDICES B & C

PROJECT TITLE ____

____

FIRM NAME ____

MAIL ADDRESS ____

CITY ____________________ STATE ______ ZIP CODE __________

AMOUNT REQUESTED $ ________ (PHASE I) DURATION ______ MONTHS (PHASE I)

OFFEROR CERTIFIES THAT:

	YES	NO
1. As defined in Section 2 of the Solicitation, this firm qualifies as a:		
1.1 Small business	☐	☐
1.2 Minority and disadvantaged small business	☐	☐
1.3 Women-owned small business	☐	☐
NOTE: 1.2 and 1.3 are not eligibility requirements for SBIR and the offeror may decline to indicate status by stating "Decline" across boxes.		
2. A minimum of two-thirds of the research and/or analytical effort for this project will be carried out within the firm if an award is made.	☐	☐
3. The primary employment of the principal investigator will be with this firm at the time of award and during the conduct of the research.	☐	☐
4 Proposals of similar content have (indicate Yes) or have not (indicate No) been submitted to another agency and the details required by Section 5.10 of the Solication are included in the proposal.	☐	☐

ENDORSEMENTS

	Principal Investigator	Corporate/Business Official
Typed Name	____________________	____________________
Title	____________________	____________________
Telephone No.	____________________	____________________

Signature of Principal Investigator ____________ Date ____________ Signature of Corporate Business Official ____________ Date ____________

PROPRIETARY NOTICE (IF APPLICABLE, SEE SECTION 5.4a, 5.5)

NOTICE: No proprietary information is included except in a Proprietary Addendum. The information (data) on pages __________ in the Proprietary Addendum section of this proposal constitute a trade secret and/or information that is commercial or financial and confidential or privileged. It is furnished to the Government in confidence with the understanding that it will not, without permission of the offeror, be used or disclosed other than for evaluation purposes; provided, however, in the event a contract is awarded on this proposal, the Government may obtain additional rights to use and disclose this information (data).

INSTRUCTIONS FOR COMPLETING APPENDIX A AND APPENDIX B

General:

To facilitate proposal processing, NASA intends to employ automated optical devices to record proposal information wherever possible. Towards this end, it is desirable, but not required, that the proposal cover sheet (Appendix A) and the project summary (Appendix B) be typed without proportional spacing using one of the following typestyles:

Courier 12 10 or 12 pitch
Courier 72 10 pitch
Elite 72
Letter Gothic 10 or 12 pitch
OCR-B 10 or 12 pitch
Pica 72 10 pitch
Prestige Elite 10 or 12 pitch
Prestige Pica 10 pitch

Please complete and ***submit the original red forms*** bound in this solicitation (not photocopies). The completed forms can then be copied for use as pages 1 and 2 of your proposal. The original red forms should be submitted in addition to the five copies of your total proposal (see section 6.2 "Physical Packaging Requirements").

Carefully align the forms in the typewriter using the underlines as a guide. The forms are printed to accommodate standard typewriting spacing.

Appendix A:

1. ***Proposal Number:*** Complete the proposal number as follows:
   a. Enter 4 digit subtopic number.
   b. Enter the last four digits of your firm's telephone number.
   c. If you are submitting different proposals under the same subtopic, enter a change letter as appropriate to differentiate proposal numbers.

Example: 1. Firm, telephone 273-8126, submits one proposal to subtopic 06.03. Proposal number is: ***06.03 8126.***

Example: 2. Firm, telephone 392-4826, submits three different proposals to subtopic 11.03. Proposal numbers are:

11.03 4826
11.03 4826A
11.03 4826B

2. ***Project Title:*** Enter a brief, descriptive title using no more than 80 keystrokes (characters and spaces). Do not use the subtopic title.
3. ***Firm Name:*** Enter full name of company submitting the proposal. If a joint venture, list company chosen to negotiate and receive contracts. If name exceeds 30 keystrokes, please abbreviate.
4. ***Address:*** Enter mail address.
   State: Enter 2 letter designation (example Maine—ME)
   Zip-Code: Enter 5 or 9 digit code
5. ***Amount Requested:*** Enter proposal amount from budget summary. Round to nearest dollar. ***Do not*** enter cents.
6. ***Duration:*** Enter proposed duration in months. If the proposed duration is other than 6 months, be sure to discuss reason in the text of the proposal.
7. ***Certifications:*** Enter Y for yes or N for no in the appropriate boxes in response to statements or questions.
8. ***Endorsements:*** The proposal should be signed by the proposed principal investigator ***and*** an official of the firm qualified to make a contractual commitment on behalf of the firm. The PI and the Corporate Official may be the same person.

Appendix B:

1. ***Proposal Number:*** Enter the same proposal number as shown on your Proposal Cover Sheet.
2. ***Project Title:*** Enter the same title as shown on your Proposal Cover Sheet.
3. ***Technical Abstract:*** Provide a summary of 200 words or less of your proposed project. The abstract must not contain proprietary information.
4. ***Potential Commercial Applications of the Research:*** Summarize the commercial potential of the project assuming the results of the proposed research or R&D are achieved.
5. ***Key Words:*** Provide no more than 8 key words descriptive of the project and useful in identifying the technology, research thrust or application of the proposed effort
6. ***Name and Address of Firm:*** Enter firm name and mail address as shown on the Proposal Cover Sheet.
7. ***Principal Investigator:*** Enter name of the Principal Investigator as shown on the Proposal Cover Sheet.

APPENDIX B - PROJECT SUMMARY

NATIONAL AERONAUTICS AND SPACE ADMINISTRATION

SBIR 90-1 SOLICITATION
(Instructions on Reverse Side)

PROPOSAL NUMBER
(TO BE COMPLETED BY PROPOSER)

	4 DIGIT SUBTOPIC NUMBER	LAST 4 DIGITS OF FIRM PHONE NO.	CHANGE LETTER
90-1	___ . ___	______	_____

AMOUNT REQUESTED: $

TITLE OF PROJECT

TECHNICAL ABSTRACT (LIMIT 200 WORDS)

POTENTIAL COMMERCIAL APPLICATIONS OF THE RESEARCH

KEY WORDS
(LIMIT 8)

NAME AND ADDRESS OF OFFEROR

PRINCIPAL INVESTIGATOR

PROPOSAL
PAGE
2

APPENDIX C - SBIR PROPOSAL SUMMARY BUDGET

NATIONAL AERONAUTICS AND SPACE ADMINISTRATION

SBIR 90-1 SOLICITATION
(Instructions on Reverse Side)

FIRM: PROPOSAL NUMBER:

PRINCIPAL INVESTIGATOR:

(See Instructions on Back of Form) TOTAL PRICE

MATERIAL: $

PERSONNEL: $

OTHER DIRECT COSTS: $

OVERHEAD: $

GENERAL AND ADMINISTRATIVE (G&A): $

PROFIT: $

TOTAL PRICE PROPOSED $

TYPED NAME AND TITLE: SIGNATURE:

THIS PROPOSAL IS SUBMITTED IN RESPONSE TO NASA SBIR PROGRAM SOLICITATION 90-1 AND REFLECTS OUR BEST ESTIMATES AS OF THIS DATE. DATE SUBMITTED

PROPOSAL PAGE NO.

INSTRUCTIONS

The purpose of this form is to provide a vehicle whereby the offeror submits to the Government a pricing proposal of estimated costs with detailed information for each cost element, consistent with the offeror's cost accounting system.

This summary does not eliminate the need to fully document and justify the amounts requested in each category. Such documentation should be contained, as appropriate, on a budget explanation page immediately following the budget in the proposal. (See below for discussion on various categories).

1. **MATERIALS —**

   a. *Materials and Supplies.* Indicate types required and estimate costs.
   b. *Publication Costs/Page Charges.* Estimate cost of preparing and publishing project results.
   c. *Consultant Services.* Indicate name, daily compensation, and estimated days of service.
   d. *Computer Services.* Include justification. Computer equipment leasing is included here. Purchase of equipment is included under OTHER DIRECT COSTS.
   e. *Subcontracts.* Include a completed budget and justify details.
   f. *Other.* Itemize and justify.

2. **PERSONNEL** — On the budget explanation page, list individually all personnel included, the requested person-months to be funded, and rates of pay (salary, wages, and fringe benefits).
3. **OTHER DIRECT COSTS** — List all other direct costs which are not otherwise included in the categories described above. For travel, address the type and extent of travel and its relation to the project. List each item of permanent equipment to be purchased, its price, and explain its relation to the project.
4. **OVERHEAD** — Specify current rate(s) and base(s). Use current rate(s) negotiated with the cognizant Federal negotiating agency, if available. If no rate(s) has (have) been negotiated, a reasonable indirect cost (overhead) rate(s) may be requested for Phase I which will be subject to approval by NASA. If a current negotiated rate(s) is (are) not available for Phase II, NASA will negotiate an approved rate(s) with the offeror. The offeror may use whatever number and types of overhead rates that are in accordance with the firm's accounting system and approved by the cognizant Federal negotiating agency, if available.
5. **GENERAL AND ADMINISTRATIVE (G&A)** — Specify current rate and base. Use current rate negotiated with the cognizant Federal negotiating agency, if available. If no rate has been negotiated, a reasonable indirect cost (overhead) rate may be requested for Phase I which will be subject to approval by NASA. If a current negotiated rate is not available for Phase II, NASA will negotiate an approved rate with the offeror.

APPENDIX D

NATIONAL AERONAUTICS AND SPACE ADMINISTRATION
SBIR 90-1 SOLICITATION

PROPOSAL CHECK LIST

Company/Name
and Address: ______________________________

____

____

Proposal Number: ______________________________

Proposal Title: ______________________________

____

CHECK

__ 1. Offeror has read Solicitation pages 1-17 and understands that proposals not meeting all requirements may be nonresponsive and may not be evaluated.

__ 2. Proposal and innovation is submitted in only one Subtopic (see Sect. 5.14-d).

__ 3. All information required by Sect. 3.3 is included in order.

__ 4. Any proprietary information, if included, is contained in a Proprietary Addendum with required Proprietary Notice (see Sect. 5.4-a).

__ 5. Certifications and Signatures on Appendices A and C.

__ 6. Period of technical performance does not exceed 6 months and funding request does not exceed $50,000.

__ 7. Proposal (including any supplementary material and/or Proprietary Addendum) contains no more than 25 - 8½ x 11 inch pages. Check list is not included in page count.

__ 8. Proposed innovation is described in first paragraph of proposal Part D-Sect. 1.

__ 9. Phase II objectives are discussed.

__ 10. Phase III potential (NASA and commercial applications) and possible approach discussed.

__ 11. Proposal package includes:

  a. Five (5) copies of Proposal
  b. Original Cover Sheet and Proposal Summary (red forms, Appendices A and B) clipped (not stapled) to Check List.

__ 12. Offeror understands that proposals must be received in NASA Headquarters by 4 p.m. EDT July 16, 1990.

Signature of person completing this Check List: ______________________________

APPENDIX E Subtopics

Field Centers[1]

No.	ARC	GSFC	JPL	JSC	KSC	LaRC	LeRC	MSFC	SSC	Subtopic
01.00										**AERONAUTICAL PROPULSION AND POWER**
01.01							■			Internal Fluid Mechanics for Aeronautical Propulsion Systems
01.02							■			Aeronautical Propulsion System Components
01.03							■			Aeronautical Propulsion System Instrumentation, Sensors and Controls
01.04							■			Novel Aeronautical Propulsion Concepts
02.00										**AERODYNAMICS AND ACOUSTICS**
02.01	■									Computational Fluid Dynamics
02.02						■				Theoretical Aerodynamics and Viscous Flow
02.03						■				Hypersonic Vehicle Aerothermodynamics
02.04								■		Rarefied Gas Dynamics
02.05								■		Plume-Induced Effects on Launch and Orbital Vehicles
02.06	■									Configurational Aerodynamics Including Vortices
02.07	■									Rotorcraft Aerodynamics and Dynamics
02.08						■				Wind Tunnel Design and Experimental Techniques
02.09						■				Wind Tunnel Instrumentation
02.10						■				Aircraft Noise Prediction and Reduction
02.11							■			Propulsion Noise Reduction
03.00										**AIRCRAFT SYSTEMS, SUBSYSTEMS, AND OPERATIONS**
03.01							■			Aircraft Ice Protection Systems
03.02						■				Aircraft Severe Weather Environment
03.03						■				Control Concepts for Fixed Wing Aircraft
03.04	■									Fully Automatic Guidance for Rotorcraft
03.05	■									Flight Research Sensors and Instrumentation
03.06	■									Aircraft Flight Testing Techniques
03.07						■				Hypersonic Flight Systems Technology
03.08	■									Very High Altitude Aircraft Technology
03.09	■									Aeronautical Human Factors and Flight Management Systems
03.10	■									Development, Testing and Verification of Flight Critical Systems
03.11	■									Integrated Aerospace Vehicle Flight Characteristics Simulation

[1] *Legend appears on page 25*

Field Centers

04.00	ARC	GSFC	JPL	JSC	KSC	LaRC	LeRC	MSFC	SSC	MATERIALS AND STRUCTURES
04.01							X			High Temperature Composite Materials Technology for Aeropropulsion Applications
04.02							X			Processing of High Temperature Composite Materials for Aeropropulsion Systems
04.03							X			Improved Fibers for High Temperature Composites for Power and Propulsion
04.04								X		Environment-Resistant Alloys for Launch Vehicle and Space Propulsion Systems
04.05							X			Computational Structural Methods for Aeropropulsion Applications
04.06						X				Composite Materials for Aerostructures and Space Applications
04.07						X				Light Alloy Metallics for Airframe Structures
04.08								X		Welding Technology
04.09						X				Nondestructive Evaluation Technology to Characterize Material Properties
04.10					X					Bond Strength of Thermal Sprayed Coatings
04.11		X								Special Purpose Materials, Processes and Testing for Space Flight Applications
04.12	X									Thermal Protection Materials and Systems
04.13			X							Adaptive Deployable Structures
04.14				X						Spacecraft Structures and Mechanisms
04.15			X				X			High Temperature Superconductors for Aerospace Applications
04.16				X						Lunar Materials Utilization

05.00	ARC	GSFC	JPL	JSC	KSC	LaRC	LeRC	MSFC	SSC	TELEOPERATORS AND ROBOTICS
05.01						X				Large Scale Telerobotoc Systems
05.02		X								Telerobotic and Biomechanical System Software Development
05.03		X								Telerobotic Electro/Mechanical Systems
05.04				X						Space Based Manipulator Mechanisms and Controls
05.05				X						Artificial Intelligence for Space Station Applications
05.06			X							Supervised Autonomous Servicing Technology
05.07							X			Space Mechanisms
05.08				X						Robotic Adaptive Grasping and Manipulation Systems
05.09								X		Mission Support Flight Robotics

Field Centers

	ARC	GSFC	JPL	JSC	KSC	LaRC	LeRC	MSFC	SSC	
06.00										**COMPUTER SCIENCE AND APPLICATIONS**
06.01						■				Engineering Computer Science
06.02		■								Software Development and Maintenance
06.03						■				Reliable Software Development
06.04	■									Knowledge-Based Systems Technologies for Aerospace Applications
06.05				■						Software Systems for Mission Planning and Flight Control
06.06	■									Computer Sciences in Computational Physics
06.07			■							Large Multiprocessor Database Technology
06.08		■								Space Flight Data Systems
06.09					■					Shuttle and Payload Ground Processing Systems
06.10	■									Optical Processing Technology
06.11						■				Analysis and Synthesis of Engineering Systems
07.00										**INFORMATION SYSTEMS AND DATA HANDLING**
07.01						■				Focal-Plane Image Processing
07.02		■								Earth Observing System Data Technologies
07.03									■	Simulation Model for Multispectral Sensors and Imaging Systems
07.04									■	Spatial Data Management and Geographic Information Systems
07.05									■	Geographic Information System Software Development
07.06						■				Information Processing Technology and Integrated Data Systems
07.07								■		Advanced Remote Sensing Database Technology
07.08		■								Heterogenous Distributed Data Management
07.09			■							Spacecraft On-Board Infromation Extraction
07.10		■								Computational Libraries for Massively Parallel Computing Systems
07.11			■							Planetary Data System Educational Software
08.00										**INSTRUMENTATION AND SENSORS**
08.01		■								Earth Atmospheric Sensing and Topographic Measurements from Space
08.02									■	Low-Cost, High Resolution, Airborne, Remote Sensing Instrumentation for Earth Sciences
08.03						■				Sensors for Aerosol and Cloud Studies
08.04		■								Laser Polarization Profiling

Field Centers

	ARC	GSFC	JPL	JSC	KSC	LaRC	LeRC	MSFC	SSC	**INSTRUMENTATION AND SENSORS (continued)**
08.05		■								Earth Atmospheric LIDAR Remote Sensing
08.06						■				Tunable Solid-State Lasers, Detectors, and LIDAR Subsystems
08.07								■		Earth Observing Sensor Development for Geostationary Orbit
08.08			■							A Cold Coronagraph for Planetary Observations
08.09		■	■							Detetectors and Detector Arrays
08.10		■								Laser Heterodyne Technology
08.11	■		■							Infrared Technology for Astronomical Applications
08.12								■		Infrared Spectroscopy with Detector Arrays
08.13			■							High-Operating-Temperature Infrared Detector Arrays
08.14			■							Submillimeter Antennas, Radiometers and Spectrometers
08.15			■							High-Field Vector Helium Magnetometer for Space Applications
08.16	■									Instrument Technology for Exobiology
08.17			■							Instrumentation for Geology
08.18		■	■							Oceanographic Instrumentation
08.19		■	■							Optical Components and Design Tools
08.20								■		Optical Fabrication and Metrology
08.21		■								Spacecraft Contamination Monitoring
08.22		■								High Resolution Charged Particle Instrumentation
08.23		■								Detectors for Gamma Ray Astronomy
08.24			■							Gamma Ray and X-Ray Spectoscopy
08.25								■		Underwater Position Three Dimensional Measuring System
08.26					■					Non-invasive Fluid Measuring Instrument

09.00 SPACECRAFT SYSTEMS AND SUBSYSTEMS

	ARC	GSFC	JPL	JSC	KSC	LaRC	LeRC	MSFC	SSC	
09.01						■				Control of Large Space Structures
09.02						■				Guidance, Navigation and Control of Advanced Space Transportation Systems
09.03		■								Digital Processor for an Earth Horizon Scanner Attitude Control System
09.04		■								Spacecraft Flight Dynamics
09.05				■						Tracking System for STS, Space Station, Lunar and Mars Missions, and Robotics
09.06				■						Space Station Crew Workstation Displays and Controls
09.07			■							Spacecraft Data Transfer Using Monolithic Microwave Integrated Circuits

Field Centers

No.	ARC	GSFC	JPL	JSC	KSC	LaRC	LeRC	MSFC	SSC	
										SPACECRAFT SYSTEMS AND SUBSYSTEMS (continued)
09.08		X								Sensor Applications of Monolithic Microwave Integrated Circuits
09.09			X							Cyrogenic Refrigeration Systems
09.10		X								Thermal Control for Unmanned Spacecraft
09.11				X						Thermal Management Systems for Manned Lunar and Planetary Missions
09.12								X		Manned Spacecraft Thermal Systems
09.13								X		Fluid Management, Leak Detection, and Fire Suppressants for Manned Missions
09.14	X									Spacecraft Plasma Environment Forecasting
09.15		X								Technologies for Long Duration Scientific Balloons
10.00										**SPACE POWER**
10.01							X			Space Energy Conversion Systems
10.02		X								Optical Coating for Aerospace Solar Cell Cover-Glasses
10.03			X							Thermal-to-Electric Conversion Technology
10.04						X				Photovoltaic-Laser Energy Converters
10.05							X			Space Electrochemical Storage Systems
10.06			X							High Specific Energy and Long Life Batteries
10.07				X						Portable Rechargeable Energy Storage for Space Station Applications
10.08							X	X		Space Power Management and Distribution
10.09				X						Electrical Power Control and Distribution Subsystems
10.10			X							Flexible Magnetic Circuit Components for Space Power
11.00										**SPACE PROPULSION**
11.01								X		Propulsion System Combustion Processes
11.02								X		Liquid Engine Internal Flow Dynamics
11.03								X		Solid Rocket Motor Technology
11.04							X			Space Propulsion Systems for Orbit-to-Orbit and Injection/Transfer Vehicles
11.05							X			Unconventional Rocket Engines for Altitude Compensation and Throttling
11.06							X			Low Reynolds Number and Plume Flows
11.07							X			Diagnostics for Chemical Rocket Engines
11.08							X			Fiber Optic Measurement Technology for Cyrogenic Liquid Propulsion Systems
11.09									X	Propulsion Ground Testing Technology

Field Centers

12.00 HUMAN HABITABILITY AND BIOLOGY IN SPACE

No.	ARC	GSFC	JPL	JSC	KSC	LaRC	LeRC	MSFC	SSC	Item
12.01				X						Medical Sciences for Manned Space Programs
12.02				X				X		Biomedical and Environmental Health Support for Manned Space Programs
12.03	X			X				X		Regenerative Life Support; Air, Water, and Waste Management
12.04	X				X					Bioregenerative Food Production
12.05	X			X				X		Human Factors for Space Crews
12.06				X						Intra-Vehicular Systems for Space Crews
12.07	X			X						Extra-Vehicular Activity
12.08	X									Human Factors for Long Duration Space Missons
12.09								X		Man-Space Systems Integration
12.10	X									Life Sciences Spaceflight Technology
12.11					X					Miniature Biomedical Telemetry Instrument
12.12								X		One-Atmosphere-Pressure Underwater Suit

13.00 QUALITY ASSURANCE, SAFETY, AND CHECK-OUT FOR GROUND AND SPACE ORGANIZATIONS

No.	ARC	GSFC	JPL	JSC	KSC	LaRC	LeRC	MSFC	SSC	Item
13.01					X					Halon Replacement for Use in Electronic Facility Fire Protection Systems
13.02					X					Portable Inductive Welder with Integral Weld Verification
13.03					X					Launch and Ground Weather Forecasting
13.04					X					Fluids and Fluid Systems Components
13.05								X		Flowmeter Test and Calibration
13.06				X						Test Facility Instrumentation and Safety Devices
13.07			X							Quality Assurance of Very Large Scale Integrated (VLSI) Circuits
13.08					X					Nondestructive Evaluation Inspection Techniques for Launch Readiness Verification

14.00 SATELLITE AND SPACE SYSTEMS COMMUNICATIONS

No.	ARC	GSFC	JPL	JSC	KSC	LaRC	LeRC	MSFC	SSC	Item
14.01				X						Communications for Manned Space Systems
14.02		X								Advanced Data Relay Satellite Systems
14.03			X							Millimeter Wave Deep Space Communications Components
14.04			X							Spacecraft Telecommunications Systems
14.05							X			Advanced Satellite Communications Systems
14.06			X							Optical Communication for Deep Space
14.07							X			Low Cost Ka-Band Ground Terminals
14.08			X							Laser Position Modulators for Optical Communications

Field Centers

15.00	ARC	GSFC	JPL	JSC	KSC	LaRC	LeRC	MSFC	SSC	MATERIALS PROCESSING, MICRO-GRAVITY, AND COMMERCIAL APPLICATIONS IN SPACE
15.01							■	■		Materials Processing in Space
15.02							■			Microgravity Science, Technology and Engineering Experiments
15.03						■				Chemical Vapor Deposition Analysis and Modeling Tools

LEGEND

ARC — Ames Research Center
Moffett Field, CA

GSFC — Goddard Space Flight Center
Greenbelt, MD

JPL — Jet Propulsion Laboratory
Pasadena, CA

JSC — Johnson Space Center
Houston, TX

KSC — Kennedy Space Center
Kennedy Space Center, FL

LaRC — Langley Research Center
Hampton, VA

LeRC — Lewis Research Center
Cleveland, OH

MSFC — Marshall Space Flight Center
Huntsville, AL

SSC — Stennis Space Center
Stennis Space Center, MS

Index

Index

About the Author

Mark Rowh is a recognized expert on the grant and contract process. Over the past 15 years he has written hundreds of grant proposals—and netted millions of dollars in state and federal awards—for a variety of institutions. He has also managed many different funded programs, and has directed workshops on grants. He is the author of five other books, as well as more than 100 articles for major publications, including *Entrepreneur* and *Women's Enterprise*. He currently serves as Director of College Relations at New River Community College in Dublin, Virginia.